WE QUIT eMAIL

KIM SPINDER

WE QUIT MAIL

Join us and regain control of your work!

Business Contact Publishers
Amsterdam/Antwerpen

© 2014 Kim Spinder
Business Contact Publishers
Translator Erwin Postma
Original title *We Quit Mail*
Cover image and interior images Marize
Engelbrecht
Cover and interior design Sander Pinkse
Boekproductie
Author photo Jeroen Bouman

ISBN 978 90 470 0787 6

www.businesscontact.nl
wequitmail.com

Contents

Introduction

The end of the year was approaching and I was struggling just to keep up with my inbox. Emails kept pouring in day after day. Whatever I did, I couldn't get through them all. Email was causing more and more stress, miscommunication, and frustration. A slight sense of despair was coming over me, as I realized that I had spent most of the year running from meeting to meeting, frenetically trying to snatch the time between to answer my emails. Finally, when I got home I would do my 'actual' work and go through the as yet unanswered emails; and still there would be a colleague the next morning asking me: 'Haven't you read my email yet?'

I felt like I was constantly playing catch-up, which was seriously denting my motivation. And I hated the fact that my schedule was being dictated by others. My personal to-do list kept on growing, left on hold while I answered my ever demanding emails. After every meeting, my inbox would be full again. I felt trapped in a vicious circle I couldn't escape. How great it would be if I could actually decide for myself when and how to communicate and collaborate with others.

I asked myself what I was actually contributing

to society. Was it of any value at all? What I wanted was to make a meaningful contribution as a professional, and have some impact on the world around me. Taking stock of the situation, I arrived at a very sad conclusion: 'I'm a master of being in meetings, writing plans and replying to emails in the meanwhile. That's it! That's all I do day in, day out. By the time I retire, my contribution to society will have amounted to next to nothing.'

The time had come. *I decided to quit email.* I made it my New Year's resolution: 'On January 1st, 2011, I will quit email. I will pull the plug on my inbox and from that point on use only online collaboration platforms.'

For the past 33 years, I have looked in the mirror every morning and asked myself: 'If today were the last day of my life, would I want to do what I am about to do today?' And whenever the answer is 'No' for too many days in a row, I know I need to change something.

STEVE JOBS, FOUNDER AND FORMER CEO OF APPLE

Sure, I was a little apprehensive at first. Would I miss out on things? Would those online collaboration platforms really do the trick? How would others react to my decision? But the overriding feeling was actually excitement; I wanted to find out if it really could benefit me, my employers, and other organizations.

Now I can finally say that quitting email has brought me even more than I had ever dared to imagine; a lot more than the mere relief of not having to open my inbox. *I could never have imagined that the way I collaborated would change so dramatically.* Not only was I now able to work much more efficiently using other tools but I also had real contact with my colleagues again.

These are the experiences I want to share, which is why I have started the We Quit eMail movement; and meanwhile the first companies and individual members have joined.[1] In this book, I will share the personal experiences and best practices of myself and others for you to take advantage of. Are you ready? Let's go!

Kim Spinder, March 2014

1

Why email doesn't do the job anymore

Email is electronic mail.

WIKIPEDIA

From a historical perspective, email is actually a rather outdated medium. While most online media have an ever shorter life span as they are overtaken by better and more user-friendly technology and platforms with a greater reach — just consider MySpace — the first email was sent back in 1971, by Ray Tomlinson, a programmer from the U.S.

The inventors of email would cry if they foresaw its slow evolution.[2]

DREW HOUSTON, DROPBOX CEO

An email is basically nothing more than a digitalized letter. Still, email as a medium has changed over the decades, starting out as a messaging service and turning into a document sharing and storage tool.[3] Actual communication between individuals has long disappeared from the top five of email functions.[4]

Email is widely used for collaboration, while it was never designed or developed with that in mind. Not surprisingly, it is precisely when using email for collaboration that we come up against its limitations.

If email was invented today, it probably would not have survived as a technology.

LUIS SUAREZ, KNOWLEDGE MANAGER AT IBM[5]

Sending an email has become the most mundane of operations. It has become so commonplace that we barely dwell on the implications. But there is indeed a downside to email. Particularly because of the huge volume of emails we have to go through, increasing numbers of people find it hard to use email effectively and it even becomes a source of stress. You know that red dot that tells you that you have 148 unread emails, that dot you keep seeing out of the corner of your eye? That dot made me restless. If you're not careful, email will control your life and be the first thing you think about in the morning and the last thing on your mind before going to sleep. I had gotten into the habit of checking my email before going to bed, which often resulted in troubled sleep as my mind would be on what I would have to do the next day. And I'm not the only one: research has shown that technology has affected our sleep. Checking your email or posting something on Facebook is very likely to lead to a restless night. A third of us sleep only five to six hours a night as a result.[6]

Technology is reciprocal. It gives you something, but it also takes something from you. Nowadays, being disconnected is a luxury.

DAAN ROOSEGAARDE, ARTIST AND INNOVATOR

In my job as a civil servant, emails flooded in every day. Whatever I did, it became harder and harder to clear my inbox. Answering emails alone was almost a full-time job. I tried everything to keep it under control: from implementing email etiquette rules to learning time-management skills such as those of the Getting Things Done method.[7] Nothing worked. I was still left with stacks of emails at the end of every day. It made me feel as if I never got any work done. I was stressed and less productive. Cutting back on the number of emails I sent seemed impossible, but in 2011 — by which time I had become an independent entrepreneur — I took the plunge.

Digital stranglehold

It would, of course, be unfair to blame it all on email. Let me be clear on one thing: I have nothing against email as a medium. I do, however, have a problem with the way we keep each other in a digital stranglehold. I was also guilty of that, circulating volumes of information by email that no one could reasonably be expected to process. I had to start with myself.

However, when you really want to change the way you collaborate with others, changing your own behavior alone is not enough, you need to get the entire organization and everyone you work with on board. And that is quite a job. For me, email has turned into a symbol of bureaucracy.

Before I finally pulled the plug on it, I made a last-ditch effort to regulate my and my co-workers' email usage. We made arrangements on how to communicate with each other. This not only confronted us with some hard facts (we turned out to be set in ways we had inherited from our predecessors), it also proved to be a lot of fun, because we had never really discussed our collaborative practices. Everyone did the things they thought were right. When we looked at what we wanted to achieve, who our emails were intended to inform, and who took the final decisions, in short: when we subjected the communication process to close scrutiny, we came to the conclusion that it could all be done a lot more efficiently.

First attempt: e-tiquette

We agreed on a 'correct' way of using email, hoping that would reduce the 'clutter' in our inboxes and enable us to empty them faster. The main points from our e-tiquette code were:

☐ Give your emails a clear subject to make it easier for recipients to scan and search emails.

☐ Describe a clear call to action: be specific on what you expect the recipient to do and by what date.

☐ Be brief: no more than five to ten lines.

Email has turned into a symbol of bureaucracy.

- ☐ Before sending an email, consider whether there is another, better way of getting your message across.
- ☐ CCing is pointless.
- ☐ BCCing is prohibited.

Second attempt: return to sender

Sticking to the above e-tiquette rules proved far from straightforward in practice, as we often lacked the required discipline because we had been doing things differently for years.

We simply couldn't get email-based collaboration right. Although we moved information around, we mostly failed to consolidate it. Email created a certain culture among the workforce that produced a lot of mutual irritation. Emails were sometimes blindly passed along without consultation, just to get rid of them (for a while). Email was also used to get actions onto someone else's to-do list, with the sender expecting the recipient to act immediately.

On top of that, the idea that emails always require an instant reply had taken root among a large section of the workforce, who would subsequently be annoyed whenever they were kept waiting for a reply. I decided to draw attention to this by returning irrelevant emails and actions that I did not want on my plate, like wrongly delivered mail, typing 'return to sender' in the subject line.

Duty to supply

In spite of these measures, my inbox was still chock-full with announcements, requests, tasks, newsletters, etc. Whenever I was out of the office for a day, and had no time to reply to emails, my inbox would be overflowing the next day. In the worst case, a project would even grind to halt as all team members were waiting for my reply. Given that we had agreed on a 'duty to supply' information instead of a 'duty to gather,' it was up to me to make sure everyone was up to date on the latest. In case of miscommunication, I, the supplier of information, was always the one getting the blame: 'You didn't CC me' or: 'I wasn't invited to that meeting.'

Email is not a messaging protocol. It's a to-do list. Or rather, my inbox is a to-do list, and email is the way things get onto it. But it is a disastrously bad to-do list.

PAUL GRAHAM, PROGRAMMER, WRITER, AND INVESTOR[8]

File 13

Your email inbox is like 'file 13'. Everything ends up in one great repository: requests, minutes for meetings, responses to questions to a group of colleagues, brief announcements, and newsletters. Sometimes people literally use their inbox as a filing cabinet. We had one colleague who did that, and whenever he was away certain knowledge was literally 'locked away' in his inbox, depriving others of access to important information.

Email bombs

And with every opinion, nuance, and addition, the archive gets fuller and fuller. Whenever our team had to make decisions, our inboxes turned into a veritable barrel bomb of emails. We would send at least sixty emails back and forth before making a decision.[9] This whole process was chaotic and produced miscommunication, as some would hit 'reply to all' while others replied privately. You had to stay on top of these emails, because you could very easily lose track of the thread and find yourself unable to make sense of the conversation. Who had replied to whom? Do they want me to do something or has a decision already been made? It sometimes took me half an hour just to figure out that an issue had already been resolved. Starting with the most recent email wasn't the answer either, because then I'd miss the underlying information.

Status unknown

What I found difficult with email is that it was never instantly clear what had priority. After all, all emails are received in the same place. The only way of finding out what requires your attention first is to open them one by one and assess what to do with them. Alongside truly important messages, my inbox would be littered with general announcements, such as: 'Jim is on sick leave,' 'birthday cake at 10am,' 'the printer is down' and 'the printer is back up,' or with common errors such as: 'Sorry, forgot the attachment,' 'this one was intended for the other Kim' or private emails that were accidentally sent to the whole team.

Unnecessary CCs and secret BCCs

And how about copying emails to colleagues who are not required to do anything with the information? CCing the whole group 'for information purposes' is often basically only a way of letting everyone know how busy you are or how great a job you are doing.

Whenever an ongoing discussion becomes heated, you suddenly see the manager's name appear in the CC line, as a way of gathering evidence against you, or to say: 'I would like the boss to weigh in.' It does, however, also work the other way round, as there are managers who want to be CCd to be able to keep an eye on things. When I, for example, would contact a director who was above my immediate superior in the pecking order, I was required to CC my superior, so that she knew I was contacting her boss.

SPENDING MOST OF YOUR DAY CHECKING EMAILS?

#WQM

So what do you do for a living?

Oh, well, I'm an Emailer.

People feel the need to include 10 other people on an email just to let them know they are being productive at work. But as a result, it ends up making those other 10 people unproductive because they have to manage that email.

CLIVE THOMPSON, AUTHOR OF SMARTER THAN YOU THINK: HOW TECHNOLOGY IS CHANGING OUR MINDS FOR THE BETTER[10]

Sometimes email conversations were escalated to superiors by BCC (Blind Carbon Copy) behind my back. What's annoying about this is that it not only leads to the proliferation of unnecessary emails, but also to scheming and mistrust, eliminating the basis of trust that is so needed for effective collaboration.

On one occasion, when I returned to work after a vacation, I spent my first few days back at work purging my inbox. Most emails were from direct colleagues who sent me emails to keep me up to date, while they knew that I was on holiday. I never understood that, because surely catching up over a coffee after a vacation is far more efficient and fun, isn't it?

Less personal contact

Email was the number 1 communication tool in our office and that automatically meant there was less personal contact. I started to feel increasingly uncomfortable with this form of communication. It became such a fixed routine that no one even gave a second thought to emailing the person they were sitting right next to. Worse still, whenever you decided to buck this trend and went over to someone's desk to discuss something, they would invariably ask: 'Can you please put that in an email?' The IT department even refused to deal with questions that were not submitted by email. What's ironic is that we used email thinking that it would speed up proceedings and boost our productivity, while in practice we would often end up sending as many as ten emails back and forth, when a simple walk over to someone's desk or a (video) call would have been a lot quicker.

Email would in some cases even cause conflict, due to the fact that it is easier to complain by email than face to face.

Also, written text is more prone to misunderstanding, as the recipient has to make do without the smile, ironic tone, or wink that people use in personal conversations to add nuance to a message. I know from experience that this can create considerable tension. Simply walking over to, or calling, my co-worker would clear the air and solve the problem within minutes, and often confirm that we had indeed misunderstood each other in emails.

Do you know what the problem is with email? It's too easy!

SIMON SINEK, AUTHOR OF *START WITH WHY*

Reset

I found that when I was at work I didn't have enough time to do my job. In the mornings, I would set targets, but incoming emails kept diverting my attention away from hitting those targets. It became harder and harder to refocus on my actual work after each interruption. But I kept checking my email, afraid I would miss out on something. It even got so bad that I would get disappointed when there were no new emails. I had become a slave to my inbox. My peers didn't always sympathize with my struggle. 'But isn't emailing what you are paid to do?' Personally, I really thought I'd been hired for something else.

Whenever I'm at a party and someone asks me what I do, I tell them I'm an 'emailer.'[11]

What if I could once more decide for myself how to do my job and what to spend my time on? Wouldn't it be great to be back in control of my own schedule? Thanks to my life hack of quitting email, I got the chance to radically break through existing patterns and personally experience that there is life after email. It felt like hitting the reset button.

2
A new mindset in the workplace

When I look back now, a few years down the line, quitting email has done more good than I could ever have imagined. There were a number of obvious quick wins: I had more time and was able to do more, and work more effectively and efficiently. After a while, however, I came to realize that there is in fact a whole new world behind We Quit eMail (WQM), one that goes beyond quitting email. WQM is merely the first step in a major overhaul of the way you work and live. In this chapter I will share my experiences and those of other WQM followers.

If you want something new, you have to stop something old.

PETER F. DRUCKER, MANAGEMENT THINKER AND AUTHOR OF *MANAGING IN THE NEXT SOCIETY* AND OTHER WORKS

The first gain: time and efficiency

On average, not sending emails gives me around two to three additional hours of extra time every day. That's what I call a quick win! It also gives my productivity a serious boost. Given that I work more efficiently, I can now run forty projects at the same time, while I would only be able to handle four before I ditched email. And I'm not the only one: 'Ever since I quit email, I do the work that used to take me forty hours in ten,' says Kevin Weijers, civil servant.[12] 'I now have time left over for things that are truly important and that's really cool!'

Three-quarters of all email is junk, and we are wasting lots of time dealing with less important messages. But it remains the mule of the information age: stubborn and strong.[13]

BARRY GILL, BUSINESS CONSULTANT AND PRODUCT MARKETING MANAGERS AT MIMECAST

According to consulting firm McKinsey, business users spend an average of 2 hours and 14 minutes a day on reading and replying to emails.[14] That is about 28 percent of a working day, or 114 emails. Harvard Business Review claimed that employees spend as much as half their working day on emails, which adds up to 111 working days a year.[15][16] Needless to say, the time savings you can achieve depend on the kind of work you do, but even a small group of employees quitting email will produce time savings across the entire organization. Research by the University of Glasgow shows that this effect is the most far-reaching when management takes the initiative.[17] When managers start cutting down on the number of emails they send, they are setting an example for their employees. Five managers halving their email output will yield 20 minutes of time savings per employee. At the average company, this could mean hundreds of working weeks gained a year.[18]

Raising awareness
As soon as people become aware of the fact that they have little control over the number of emails they receive, but *do* have control over the number of emails they send, they will in virtually all cases immediately and drastically cut back on the number of emails they send.

It is actually quite strange that management and change experts focus so little attention on email usage. In these times of companies looking for better forms of collaboration and smarter work organization, We Quit eMail is an extremely useful tool. 'Organizations are better off dropping methods such as Lean and turning to We Quit eMail instead,' says Lucien Engelen, Director of the REshape Center at Radboud University Medical Center. He calculated how much time the Medical Center could save by quitting email. Every month, 750,000 emails were sent and 1.2 million received.[19] Assuming every recipient spends 1 minute dealing with each incoming email (which is not a lot of time, considering some will have attachments), this will cost the organization 12,500 hours a month, which equals around 100 full-time positions a year, spent on dealing with emails alone. If the number of emails every employee has to read were reduced by one every day, this would free up eight full-time jobs' worth of time.' A lot of valuable time is wasted at the hospital due to email. Imagine that time were available for patient care.

A different form of collaboration

Collaboration requires communication, but email has turned out to fall short in that department. Social media platforms are, in fact, much better suited to that role: the time spent on exchanging information across a company can be reduced by as much as 25 to 30 percent by using social media.

But this is merely the first step. Quitting email heralds a new way of communicating and collaborating, where leadership and responsibility are shared.

Self-managing teams

Online collaboration ensures employees are better informed and their contributions more targeted, as they share knowledge and ownership of what they are working on. All information is available in the agreed place and everyone has access to it, giving all stakeholders insight into progress and the opportunity to make a meaningful contribution and, wherever necessary, go that extra mile. The traditional hierarchy makes way for self-managing teams, in which natural leaders are given the room to show what they can do and excel. As members of these teams, employees are responsible for what

Suffering From a Flooded Inbox?

#WQM

they do, which fosters personal leadership. In the old structure, employees were stifled in effectively deploying their creativity and talent. Now, everyone can contribute based on their qualities, forging mutual understanding and appreciation. Consequently, departments no longer have to defend their actions with a meaningless 'that just happens to be how we work.'

We now, for example, work in an online group where everyone has access to all information. Members post updates or questions that all other members will be able to see. Team members respond to each other and help each other, building a strong team spirit. Back in the age of email, these communications would all be routed through me, the project manager. I would end up spending a large chunk of my time coordinating and emailing information. Project members would put their questions to me by email, and have to wait for my answer before they could proceed. Posting questions on an online platform helps everyone and eliminates the wait for my response. Knowledge is no longer withering away in our inboxes.

WQM also recalibrates the role of managers. Email goes well in a hierarchical organization, where all information flows run through managers, who decide what must be done, and how, and by whom. Only managers have access to all information and have the final say on what information will be shared. Some employees will get more information than others, and sometimes someone will get more information than they need. Questions from employees are submitted to the team manager and then make their way to the next manager up, who will in turn pass them on to their staff, and the subsequent answer will follow the same route back to the employees.

Making information available to everyone, online collaboration will also enable communication between team members without the intervention of a manager. 'Don't leave me out of the loop' or 'that has to run through me' are a thing of the past. Employees now ask and answer questions between themselves and give each other feedback. They can make the most of the information available across the organization.

Collective intelligence

The advantage of online networks is that they allow users to harness collective intelligence far more easily than when using email. It enables employees to determine for themselves which subjects they are interested in, and what they want

I had become a slave to my own inbox.

to collaborate on. In the words of Marnix Bolkestein, Head of Enforcement, Housing Authority, City of Amsterdam: 'Optimum collaboration and innovation is something that everyone wants. But many people never stop and think about what exactly that means in terms of managing people. We currently often pigeon-hole people. But that way you are only maintaining the old culture. Luckily, this new way of working is increasingly gaining ground in organizations.'

The benefits will not be restricted to your own organization. During the early stages of a project, you may lack a good idea of who else is active in the same field. Outsiders may also have useful ideas and they may be willing to contribute. By using social media, you can very rapidly expand your network and tap the crowd, both within and outside of your organization. The online *JongGR* community, for example, was set up to get young scientists to contribute to innovation in the area of health care policy.[20] And in an effort to make it easier for civil servants to swap jobs, Open Lab uses social media to organize speed dates between civil servants and public sector employers.[21]

Connections

WQM establishes more connections across the organization, as online and offline collaboration mutually reinforce each other. Before, as a project manager, I had the best overview of who was working on what. I would sometimes urge employees to get in touch with peers at other sites that were working on the same subjects, but in practice only a few would actually do so. They often didn't know whom to contact. Through online collaboration, different sites can see what everyone is working on and instantly respond to each other's activities. They can share issues and help each other progress.

The great thing about online collaboration is that you also get spontaneous help from others, sometimes from unexpected sources, as employees can easily find each other online. Making contact with other disciplines and organizations is equally simple, making it far easier for employees to launch projects themselves.

Working together in groups across departmental and organizational boundaries also helps counter compartmentalization and fragmentation. Everyone reports on their progress and can respond to the progress of others. This also leads to more personal contact. Employees will be quicker to go and see each other, because they already know each other online. I am finding that I am more likely to speak to others, both on business and personal matters. When I see online that my colleague ran a marathon at the weekend, I will congratulate her by the coffee machine on Monday morning. In the past, I would probably not even have known she had run a marathon.

Thanks to WQM, colleagues who spend little time at the office will find it easier to acquire a sort of profile. Employees in the office would often complain that they had no idea what field staff members did all day, but the online collaboration platform now lets field staff share knowledge with the office-based organization by posting photos of what they are doing, inviting others to respond.

This has brought a lot of positivity to the atmosphere at work, and eliminated the complaining.

The information co-workers now share is different from what they used to share by email, and that is down to the medium they use. It would have been odd to email field work photos to everyone, but posting them on Twitter is very normal. That is the power of online social platforms. One fine example comes from the local authorities in Amsterdam, where field staff share pictures of what they encounter or are working on. 'The other day, our field staff was involved in an exciting operation,' says Marnix Bolkestein (Head of Enforcement). 'Employees in the field kept everyone back at the office informed by posting photos and updates, making us all feel part of the operation. When our field staff returned to the office at the end of the day, they were welcomed with cheers and applause. I've never seen anything like it in all the years I've worked here. Employees are visibly more content and happier with this new form of collaboration and communication.'

Different collaboration

Quitting email has greatly changed the way people at departments, on teams, and on projects work together. Responsibility for hitting targets used to lie with the team leader. Although everyone would contribute on an individual level, only the team leader could see the bigger picture. Only at work meetings would co-workers find out about what others were doing. By using an online collaboration platform, you are creating more mutual involvement, as everyone can see their impact within the greater unit. People feel responsible for the success of the project as a whole, and not only for their own patch. This, in turn, also makes the work more fun. Marnix Bolkestein continues: 'Operations by our field staff lead to tasks that other departments need to follow up on. Seeing as colleagues have taken care of all the preparations, the work they do will also feel more valuable. Everyone can see how they are a link in the chain. From field service to administration, every task is crucial in doing a job. This produces greater team spirit within the workforce, and makes that everyone is more committed to each other.'

Only when you quit email, you become aware of just how individual that medium is. Creating an online group will forge a culture of teamwork. First ask 'Who will be involved in this project?' and then invite them to join the group. Also, when you are collaborating in a chain, and there are some people who will only have a role in the project at a later stage, you can invite them to follow the communications so that they will already be 80% up to speed when it is their turn to contribute. This will prevent miscommunication and build understanding for the choices made along the way. With all project stakeholders now living the entire project together, there is greater empathy and willingness to help each other when something doesn't work out. The responsible board members will also feel greater involvement when they can participate online, as they can track the process and progress, and experience how the group is working. Monthly bilaterals are no longer needed, the overall assessment will generally be more positive, and project team members hugely appreciate the commitment shown by board members. Managers informally monitor progress, respond to issues, and give compliments when appropriate. This kind of interim feedback and these signs of appreciation are very motivating to employees, especially when coming from the higher echelons of management.

A different role for managers

As a manager, this new way of working gives you more time to focus on what really matters, while also allowing you to facilitate your staff in doing a good job. You suddenly find yourself with time to have coffee with someone and calmly go over the work. But online collaboration also changes the way you coach your employees. Team members coach each other within the network, instead of managers doing so individually. This is because of the unique dynamics of working within an online group, where members correct and motivate each other. Together, you build a positive and creative atmosphere, one in which everyone wants to be part of the group, because that's where the action is. Marnix Bolkestein on this aspect: 'I've noticed that, as a manager, you are much better off going down the road of online collaboration. When you get that to work smoothly at your department, it will be far more effective than any personal conversation with your employees. Being part of a team is very important to people, and determines whether they enjoy coming to work. If they enjoy working on a result together, they will get started with a positive frame of mind. You, as a manager, will then also have a much better idea of where you should intervene. What's remarkable is that whenever I think it's time I intervened, someone else in the group often already has. I see myself as a small engine firing on these dynamics. You do have to invest in online collaboration and set the tone, otherwise you run the risk of creating a negative atmosphere. There is no room for negativity, there is a positive vibe. Other than that, the group runs on its own. My personal tip: dare, from a management position, to create a group, discuss the targets, and work toward a result. In my case, the online platform Yammer has proved to be a winning factor. It creates a better mutual bond, you get a lot more things done, and you communicate better. It has also brought greater awareness of what we are working to achieve, of the fact that eventually we are all working for the citizens of Amsterdam.'

Knowledge is no longer withering away in our inboxes.

Online collaboration changes the dynamics. In the past, we would allocate pending tasks based on employees' positions. In an online group, people can take initiative and display creativity, which is precisely what email used to stifle. We are now seeing that job profiles are actually restrictive. WQM makes it possible to bestow responsibilities lower down in the organization. Instead of telling employees what to do, you give them space to work in a more 'organic' fashion. It may prove tricky for the manager, but you have to (learn to) let go. In your new role, you are a facilitator instead of a controller. Professionals take the lead themselves, distributing the work between themselves, based on what they like, want to learn, or availability. Employees look beyond their job descriptions or titles, doing what it takes to move the project to the next level. They are, as a result, making much better use of their strengths. When you limit people to tasks that fit within their job description, you are failing to tap their full potential. 'Having worked with online collaboration for a while now, I realize that we, managers, largely assign tasks to individuals, which results in dreary bureaucratic execution,' says Marnix Bolkestein. When you quit email and go looking for alternatives, there is one recurring question: what are we working to achieve? This makes quitting email an ideal opportunity for managers to re-engage with their staff and talk about the way of working and the organizational change. It makes it easier to talk about why you do the things you do, the way you do.

Focus on progress

I used to be a fervent advocate of a result-driven work attitude. My management style sought to steer employees toward results, and as deadlines neared I would chase up staff members to get them to deliver on time. The downside was that my employees would postpone those tasks that would not yield instant results, eventually causing them to be pressed for time or have other priorities.

In my case, online collaboration brought about a shift from result-driven management to progress-based management. This is, in fact, a very logical shift: when you keep an eye on progress every day or every week, you will eventually arrive at the end result automatically. The key is therefore to ensure there is progress. Whenever I noticed that progress was stalling, I would ask myself how I could facilitate the group to take another step.

This developed into a different approach: we now work out the tasks for the coming thirty days in concrete terms, in order to be able to work together when the time for a specific task comes. These tasks are tracked online, so that everyone is aware of the latest state of affairs. We share progress through weekly online updates, celebrating our achievements online. As a result, everyone is eager to contribute to the targets. In the old situation, I would often have to chase up employees. Now, team members call each other to account when someone hasn't done what they were supposed to do. Everyone knows when something has to be done in order for someone else to be able to continue. This shared responsibility makes that everyone feels committed to making the project a success.

Cutting it up

We cut large projects of, for example, one thousand days up into smaller chunks of one hundred days. When there is progress every one hundred days, we will gradually get closer to the end result. The advantage of this is that you don't have to write extensive action plans that cover all eventualities within a project, but instead can get started right away. When there is insufficient progress after one hundred days, you can intervene or even pull the plug on the project.

A new mindset

When email ceases to be your primary channel, you will be triggered to think about how you communicate. You will develop a new mindset, changing the way you view your work. Things you took for granted suddenly become challenges. It wasn't until I quit email that I noticed that many organizations are dominated by a culture of control and mistrust. This is also the origin of the CC culture, which produces so many unnecessary emails. Mistrust is not resolved by CCing managers in emails, but rather by making clear arrangements, facilitating knowledge sharing, and most importantly, by working together based on trust.

A decision to change the way you communicate is not instantly welcomed by everyone. Whenever I, for example, would agree to something with someone face to face, they would invariably ask me to confirm by email. And arrangements made over the phone often had to be confirmed with a text message. People seek security in writing. Email is used to document things, because we apparently don't really trust each other. It gives us proof, so that we can cover our backs, or pass the buck whenever we can't handle something.

I probably always used to confirm these agreements by email without a second thought. But since I could no longer do that, I was forced to rethink our form of collaboration, and that is when it struck me that questions are often motivated by mistrust. Kevin Weijers, the aforementioned civil servant, on this point: 'Employees use email to cover their backs, or to be able to say: "Yes, but you said this." I have found that I prefer not to work like that. I want people to trust that I will do as I say. And if I ever don't, you can talk to me about it.

Mistrust is not solved by CCing managers.

Lack of trust leads to us doing things twice. This suddenly becomes clear when you quit email.' Tjitske Poelsma, Advisor at the Dordrecht municipality, recognizes this: 'Colleagues say: "Please put it in an email, and it's agreed." That's doing the same thing twice, because we are already agreeing on it now, aren't we? It is actually quite odd that people still want it in an email as well. If I were to fail to do what I agreed to do, you can just come over, and we'll talk about it.'

Quitting email requires a culture change. People seek security in email and are afraid to personally call each other to account. However, trust is not something you can record in emails and documents. Emmaly Sibbes, Policy Advisor at the Dordrecht municipality: 'Colleagues were unable to answer when I asked them: "Why do you want me to email it, we've just agreed on it, haven't we? Don't you trust my word? That's quite strange, because surely you trust what people say instead of whatever it says in an email?" Sometimes people seek that safeguard in advance, without even knowing the other person. I don't want to work that way.'

More focused

Quitting email inspired me to take a critical look at how I work and communicate. Only now do I see how much time I wasted on things that didn't even matter. My focus is now on the task I'm working on, instead of scattered as I try to multitask. I used to check and respond to emails in between other tasks, anytime and anywhere. Now, my full focus is on one project before I move on to the next. This clear focus in my work has given me the time to, for example, go to the gym in the evenings, because I now hit my daily targets.

Emmaly Sibbes concurs: 'Quitting email helps you reflect on the contents of your job. What are the trends and developments? What challenges do we have to deal with? It's a sad indictment of modern communication when emailing becomes all you do during a working day, and I don't want that to happen to me. We should establish actual contact between people instead of retreating behind our computer screens, writing memos, and distributing these by email. Thanks to new media, we can strike up new relationships and join groups in society for more effective communication.' Ditching email has put me back in charge of my work. The first few email-free weeks were a real breath of fresh air. At the start of the day, I could decide for myself what I was going to do that day. I felt less stressed, as I was no longer hounded by the feeling that there were important emails in my inbox I should be reading. Research has already corroborated that people who quit email at work are less susceptible to stress and more productive.[22]

I have regained control of my diary and my time. Everything comes together in one place, boosting my productivity and liberating me from having my days dictated by my inbox. This is, however, conditional on you agreeing with your peers on when something has to be done by and where to store all the information. When I, for example, have to complete a number of tasks by Friday afternoon, I will decide for myself what I will be working on at any time before the deadline. On Friday afternoon, I will then log on to the online collaboration platform, look at what my colleagues have done, and upload my contribution. After that, I log off, and move on to the next task.

All in one place

I used to get emails about all my projects every day, even about low-priority projects. I would open these emails to assess whether any action on my part was required, meaning that I had already been dragged into it, and would not have time left to do what I really should have been doing. Besides, I often didn't know what to do with an email I had just opened. How would I be able to find it again when I actually needed it? Of course, I sometimes also decided not to open emails, but as the deadline neared, I would still be forced to go through my entire inbox to piece together all the information and attachments, open and assess all replies, only to conclude that half of the information was no longer valid.

Now, everything is kept in one place online, making it easy for me to see whether there is anything I need to do with it. I only delve into the information for a project when I actually have the time to work on it. As a result, I decide when I work on something, instead of others dictating what I do.

When you stop using email, the start of your day changes drastically, greatly increasing your productivity. That is where Tjitske Poelsma gained the most time: 'I used to get coffee in the morning and check my email. Two hours later, I would not have done any of the tasks I had initially set out to do. Now, I first ask myself: what needs to be finished, what's most important? That is what I work on first, and after that I have time left over for communication. Quitting email has completely overhauled my work approach.'

No more multitasking
Having banished many of the distractions, I have found that I am better able to focus and work on a task for two to three hours straight. I multitask less, and am more productive. I used to check my email at least every hour, and would always be distracted from what I was doing. Doing three things at the same time made me inefficient. It may have seemed as if I was working faster because I immediately dealt with everything that was dropped on my plate, but I wasn't. Whenever you are distracted, and squeeze in something else, you need some time to get back into what you were initially doing. That is where a lot of time is lost. Aside from that, you often first revisit what you had already done, meaning that you are not actually making any progress.

I now make a list every morning of all the tasks I want to complete, and I work on those tasks with undivided attention. Checking off completed tasks on that list really gives me a fantastic feeling! Work gets done so much more quickly, and you get a real sense of satisfaction when you have done everything you set out to do. Kevin Weijers: 'I have regained actual control over what I am doing. And I would go so far as to say that I am now more productive than ever before. It's a bizarre experience, because I used to think answering five emails at 10pm was a sign of productivity.'

Innovation

Quitting email has given me tremendous peace of mind, not only at work, but also when I want to relax. I am now much better able to relax, knowing I don't have a throbbing email inbox calling for my attention. This actually comes with a very welcome side-effect: peace of mind is conducive to innovative thought. I basically lacked the peace of mind I needed to really do a good job. Back in the days when I was still spending so much time on emails, my working days were carbon copies of each other. To break through the routine, stepping back from your job is exactly what you need to do. I do have time for reflection now. According to Johan Braeckman, Professor of Philosophy at Ghent University in Belgium, we never get a break.[23] 'Our minds skip from one email temptation on our smartphones to the next every couple of seconds, making us incapable of creative thought. Our brains never get a moment of respite, and have to process so many stimuli that we lose our focus. We are expected to do more and more, and faster, and there is no escaping it. Virtually everybody is burdened by the drawbacks of this reality.'

Satisfaction

What do I really find important in my job and what value am I adding? Prior to quitting email, I would often ask myself that. Due to the fact that I am now better able to concentrate, I get a lot more satisfaction out of my work. Ridding myself of email has given me the time to reflect now and again, and with that the opportunity to tap a new source of creativity. I am basically taking a run-up that allows me to work faster. I enjoy my work a lot more, because it is now more of an outlet for my personal skills, and I feel more valuable than before. And I'm not the only one. 'I now have more time to talk to my people over the phone or over a coffee,' says Lucien Engelen of the Radboud REshape Center. 'It has literally eliminated the noise from the communication process that absorbed so much of my attention. On the one hand, I'm getting more sleep, and on the other the peace of mind I need be able to focus on the things that really matter.'

People seek security in writing.

No longer addicted

Quitting email made me realize how addicted I was to all my devices. I would obsessively check my email all day every day. The sad fact was that I couldn't just 'do nothing,' not even for a second. Even when I was at a restaurant with friends, I would keep an eye on my display or quickly grab my phone when my companions were away from the table. I would then check whether I had any new emails and be disappointed if I didn't. And when I did, I would quickly scan the contents, even though there was absolutely nothing I could do with the information at that specific moment. For the rest of the evening, I would then be thinking about all the things I had to do, making me restless and stressed, and, to be honest, spoiling my evening. Ever since I kicked the email habit, I have become more mindful of this effect. I have a new personal policy of not reading something when I can't do anything with the information at that moment anyway. I have disabled all new message alerts for my social media accounts. Checking the latest updates while at a bar with my friends is therefore a thing of the past.

The reason why we receive so many emails is that we reply to all of them.
SIMON SINEK

Looking back, I am so glad this has changed thanks to WQM. I live in the moment so much more now, instead of spending time with someone while at the same time communicating with people elsewhere. Sherry Turkle so aptly referred to this as being alone together.[24] 'It's actually quite strange,' says Emmaly Sibbes, 'I always used to check my email when I went to bed. And that is precisely when you can be sure there is nothing you will do with the information you receive. All it will do is make you tense, as you know what you've got coming at you in the morning. Only now do I see that's what used to happen.'

> *What is so seductive about texting, about keeping that phone on, about that little red light on the BlackBerry, is that you want to know who wants you.*
>
> SHERRY TURKLE, PROFESSOR OF SOCIAL STUDIES OF SCIENCES AND TECHNOLOGY AT MIT AND AUTHOR OF *THE SECOND SELF* AND *ALONE TOGETHER*

Buried Under Hundreds of Emails?

#WQM

People who have quit email all say they more consciously choose when to consume information. They feel less stressed, are more composed, and enjoy more quality time with their family, without interruptions from incoming emails in the weekend. Kevin Weijers: 'I used to have my eyes on my display screen all day, checking for updates. Ever since I quit email, I don't do that anymore. This made me realize that I had become unable to just do nothing. I have now switched off all notifications on my cell phone. Funnily enough, I now get annoyed by others who keep checking their phone. I was at a concert the other day, and there were people there who couldn't leave their phone in their pocket for more than five minutes. Perhaps I was like that before, but I now abhor that kind of behavior.'

More social contact

Whenever I talk to people about We Quit eMail, they often express a fear of being out of the loop. 'Will I still be connected socially? Won't I miss out on all kinds of things? Will the world continue without me?' I must admit, I had this fear myself at first. 'How will people get hold of me? Won't I miss out on jobs?' This fear was unfounded. In fact, I am much more informed than before, and have better contact with the people I work with. Contacts used to be brief and superficial. Now, I talk to people at the coffee corner or on social media. Lucien Engelen has the same experience: 'Now I've quit email, I actually feel I don't miss out on anything anymore, I'm better connected than ever before, and I have more and better contact with people than before.' 'I suffered from FOMO (Fear Of Missing Out),' Kevin Weijers also admits. 'But it wasn't so bad in the end. I don't feel I'm missing out at all. Quite the contrary: I'm very up to date on what's going on. When I run into people, they ask me something, noticing how much quicker direct face-to-face contact is. Precisely by going for more personal contact instead of sending an email, I now get to talk to more people, allowing me to arrange and agree on things in less time. I now hear the following phrases a lot: "Now I have your ear, what do you think about this..." and "It was useful that I could talk to you..." My colleagues were quietly jealous of me for quitting email!'

WQM has really made my job a lot more fun. I have more personal contact, which also leads to better collaboration, making our work more effective and efficient. Back when everything was still handled by email, I missed the social element and felt the bond between me and my colleagues weaken. We barely saw each other, and whenever we ran into each other, all we would say was: 'I emailed you the other day.' I am far more connected now, because the online platform lets me track everything my colleagues do. But collaboration has certainly not only been strengthened in the digital realm. We also have more coffees together and really engage in conversation, instead of sending an email to the person sitting right next to us. Emmaly Sibbes: 'We are saving a lot of time. Normally, I would send huge swathes of prose for a pre-holiday handover, an email of about 4 sheets of A4-size paper that would easily take me an hour to draft. Now, I have a coffee with my colleagues for ten minutes and it's done. You do need to have faith in people, because you cannot revert to email.'

Emotional information

Simon Sinek, author of *Start With Why*, claims that although email is a handy information sharing tool, it cannot handle emotional information.[25] 'Whenever you get the question "What do you think about my idea" in an email, do not respond by email.

This is an emotional question, and email is a rational tool. Get up from behind your desk, walk thirty yards over to the person's cubicle and answer the question. In doing so, you will create a personal relationship with your co-worker, and the information will be better received. If your co-worker is more than walking distance away, pick up the phone, and give him or her your feedback verbally. The chance of someone misunderstanding an email and getting upset is considerable, and if that happens, you still have to go over there or call, so you might as well do that right away. It is faster, easier, and better.'

Never email when you can call
Never call when you can video chat
Never video chat when you can face to face[26]
DIEGO RODRIGUEZ, PARTNER AT IDEO

Fewer and different meetings

The way I have work meetings and consultations with my colleagues has also changed since I quit email. My diary used to be filled with meetings that were actually of very little real value. As part of the switch to online collaboration, I have also scrapped fixed work meetings altogether. Instead of those scheduled meetings, we now have spontaneous get-togethers, where we share ideas and help each other. The great thing about this kind of informal meeting is that we really have time and attention for each other and spend it on meaningful things, instead of 'having a meeting for the sake of having a meeting.'

Creative processes run much smoother when those involved have personal contact, and spontaneous meetings and conversations stimulate innovation enormously. In the old days of email and traditional meetings, there simply was no time

They are viewing the new world through old glasses.

for that. Everyone just wanted to get through the agenda of the meeting as quickly as possible, or would spend the meeting doing their email. Tjitske Poelsma at the Dordrecht municipal authority also found the social impact of quitting email to be one of the major benefits: 'You suddenly start speaking to many more people, which brings so much content to the surface that you would never have unearthed by email. It's also a more pleasant way of working, with more personal contact. The fear of missing out has disappeared. You start looking for new ways of sharing information. It has become easier to work together, because we all update the agenda for departmental meetings in online shared folders. We are responsible for that, which makes us more active. Consultations are now really about something. In fact, we sometimes cancel meetings when there is nothing to discuss. It's a more pleasant and easier way of collaborating than by email. I'm fairly sure we will not go back to our old ways.'

As it turns out, quitting email can lead to a drastic reduction in the number of meetings. Marnix Bolkestein has seen this happen: 'We used to get together every two weeks, with me chairing proceedings. At every meeting, people would bring their problems to the table, which would subsequently be placed on an action list. Two weeks later, we would be talking about the exact same things. Ever since we switched to the online platform, we have stopped having scheduled departmental meetings. There's no need for these kinds of meetings anymore, as we consult with each other through the platform as and when needed. Only when there is a problem do you convene a small meeting and solve it together. We have adopted a more ad-hoc meeting style. These meetings are not attended by everyone at the department, but only by those employees who have a stake in the issue at hand. We only have a meeting when the online discussion shows there is a need for it. If not, people will sort things out between themselves. They do need to have personal contact, but you do not need to have work meetings for that. Although it gives you a sense of security to have regularly scheduled work meetings, the problems that need to be addressed are often left to fester.'

What I personally like about it is that I have more quick chats with people, because it is often a lot quicker to go over to someone's desk or (video) call them. A lot of people think sending an email is quicker, but in reality emailing is actually more time-consuming, such as when someone asks several questions in one email and keeps getting only half answers in return. Kevin Weijers: 'Someone emails a question on Monday. Drafting that email took him at least ten minutes. I read his email and reply. He reads my answer on Tuesday, but it is not quite what he wanted to know. He replies to my reply and I send him another reply. By now, it's Wednesday. We run into another, we have a quick five-minute chat about it, and it's problem solved. Because we initially tried to solve it by email, we have put in far more time than we needed to.' It is as if we have subconsciously accepted that email is time-consuming, stress-producing, and annoying, but just part of the job.

Settling into a new pattern

At many organizations, email is the primary means of communication. Attempts to stop using it in favor of an online collaboration platform therefore need to be given time to work. Initially, everyone is excited about it, and most of the workforce spontaneously joins the initiative. However, due to the fact that the new medium has not yet been incorporated into 'their system,' they soon revert to email. Only a few die-hards continue to post messages on the platform, but the rest thinks: 'Don't you have anything better to do, just get to work.' And yet these early adopters are crucial: they can be the ones who make this new way of working spread across the organization like wildfire. After all, they have first-hand experience of the benefits. They can show others how to use the online platform and make people excited about working without email.

Daily usage
Online collaboration will only truly take off when employees start using the online platform as part of their day-to-day activities, such as by creating a group for a department or a team, so that the platform will actually help you do a better job. This requires a different way of working, and it will therefore take some time for people to incorporate this into their daily routines. The sensible thing is to take this time instead of going back to email as soon as the going gets tough.

Email is so deeply rooted in our psyche that it is a huge challenge to get people to switch to a new form of collaboration.

THE NEXT WEB[27]

It helps if the board of the company is on the online platform and for HR to create accounts for new hires on their first day. 'Our board of directors is also active on our Yammer platform,' Lucien Engelen points out. 'New employees are all invited to join a group that we use to keep everyone posted about what is going well and what bottlenecks there are. It has come about organically, and you can see that it works when people go to the trouble of occasionally posting things for the group. This allows you to be inspired by others and streamline innovation at your organization. Eventually, smarter working becomes systemic and all you know. Whenever you launch a new project, the first thing you will do is set up an online group.'

Smarter working will eventually become systemic.

Resistance

Marnix Bolkestein: 'Sometimes the decision to go online is met with resistance. When you say: "Let's quit email," a number of people will immediately go on the defensive. These will also be the people who complain about not being informed because they have not received anything by email. I then use an information meeting to let them know that we now communicate through a platform. Skeptics will then join in as well, albeit after overcoming a certain level of hesitation. It all starts in the part of the organization where people adopt the new medium, from where it will gradually spread. I recently told my staff: "By next week we need a proposal that is supported by everyone." Thanks to the online platform, people can respond to the proposal quickly and easily, far more directly and effectively than by email.'

Employees who are used to communicating by email are afraid to let go of old habits or certainties, or they think of the online collaboration platform as yet another thing they have to keep checking, while they are already extremely busy with their day-to-day activities.

I am also seeing a digital skills gap form, as some people lack digital skills. Someone once mailed me a printed email, simply because she knew of no other way of getting the document to me. An increasing number of organizations are requiring their staff to have certain digital skills, and these skills will be part of the skill set for many jobs in the 21st century. Many employees still have to learn how to successfully work and share knowledge with others online. These employees are often also the skeptics: 'Would that not be moving the problem from your inbox to online media, such as Facebook, Twitter, Yammer, or LinkedIn?' They are viewing the new world through old glasses.

Emmaly Sibbes: 'It is a truly different mindset, a step change. Change is often met with incomprehension and mistrust. Colleagues sometimes tenaciously hang on to the old. Anyone can acquire digital skills, even my grandmother. Besides, online tools are increasingly easy to use. It is first and foremost a new way of thinking, and that is where the generation gap comes to the fore. Older generations have a different frame of reference. They remember the days when you still had to hand write letters, they made the major step of switching to Word for that, and now they have to assimilate yet another development. This is asking a lot of their capacity for change, contrary to younger staff, who already use online platforms to maintain social relations in their private lives. Key enabling conditions for quitting email are digital skills and self-reliance. There is no ultimate tool and IT does not provide an answer to everything. You have to dare to experiment and find tutorials online to learn how something works. You really don't have to know it all by heart. We count on people to be able to cope, but some may need a helping hand. I do worry sometimes about how to get the older employees on board.'

50 percent of the old guard will leave within two years, because they struggle to adapt to a system that will not let them play God.

MORNING STAR

It helps to just go ahead and take the first steps, so that they experience the difference and can think about the possibilities in a new way. Besides, many young staff members enjoy helping their co-workers get started. I'm not saying that new technology is 'the exclusive preserve of the young,' or that young people are by definition all equally good at it. In my experience, people sometimes need to cross a threshold to be able to learn new skills and to use new tools. They often blindly exclaim: 'I don't know how any of that works!' But you don't have to. I myself am by no means a tech whiz.

Have you also reached the point where you are ready to take that first step and experience the benefits? If so, follow the five steps in the next chapter and discover how you can do your job without email.

3

Toward a life without email in no more than five steps

I am always on the lookout for life hacks, ways of breaking through a fixed routine or particular way of working to boost my productivity and efficiency.[28] Quitting email is a life hack, as it will break you out of the email rut and lead to more efficient communication.

I must admit: it's fairly daunting to quit email. I had all kinds of thoughts race through my head: 'Will I not miss out on important info or jobs? How will my co-workers react?' The worst-case scenario would be complete isolation and losing my job, which would be pretty unpleasant, I agree, but not the end of the world. I decided to take the leap, because I was convinced that I was not making the most of my skills.

It always seems impossible until it's done.

NELSON MANDELA

How to put it into practice

What is the right moment to quit email? The first few days are unnerving and awkward. You suddenly find yourself in the middle of a voyage of discovery. Like many other WQM followers, I experienced quitting email as a form of kicking a habit. 'On the last day of email, I tried to get all kinds of things done,' says Emmaly Sibbes (Dordrecht municipality). 'After a bad night's sleep, I went to work as nervous as a turkey at Christmas. I had my doubts, even considered not going ahead with it, but I did. I really felt the fear of missing out on things, and did have quick peeks at my inbox during the first week. But as you see the volume of emails diminish, you become more relaxed. The alderman, for example, started contacting me on Twitter. Getting this kind of support felt good, as others realized that my move was actually benefitting the organization as a whole.'

I got a wide range of responses when I quit email. Some people were curious, asking how I was going to communicate with friends. 'Well, through WhatsApp, Facebook, or Skype, or simply over a cup of coffee,' I would reply. As you would expect, there were also people who tried to convince me that they really couldn't work without email, while others confessed: 'I stopped reading my emails long ago.' Some clients were critical of my move: 'Sure, good for you, but now *I* have a problem!' Even so, the fact that I soon started experiencing the first tangible results strengthened my resolve in persevering with this life hack.

Toward a life without email in five steps

Many people I speak to say they would love to cut down on their email usage, but don't know how to shape collaboration without email. Are you also ready to take that first step and experience the benefits? If so, follow these five steps. The method you choose in step 1 will determine the subsequent steps.

1 Choose the We Quit eMail method that best suits you.
2 Scan your inbox.
3 Start sending fewer emails.
4 Make new work arrangements.
5 Choose your tools.

Step 1: Choose the We Quit eMail method that best suits you

There are various ways of quitting email, ranging from stopping gradually to going cold turkey. Study these strategies and choose the one that best suits you and your organization. Run your plans by people you communicate and work with a lot, and do this well in advance, letting them know when you will join We Quit eMail.

We have defined the following WQM methods:
I.   Pulling the plug, making a clean break
II. Eliminating email step by step
III. Going on an email diet
IV. Stop gradually
V.   Start small: as a department, team, or project

These methods will be detailed in the following sections.

WQM method I: Pulling the plug, making a clean break

This is the method I chose, because an email diet turned out to be ineffective for me, as my inbox sucked me back in only a few days into my email diet, taking me back to where I started. For me, there was only one way to go: cold turkey. It made me more creative in finding other communication channels. When you allow yourself to still send the occasional email, you will soon revert to your old email ways.

Set a quitting date in your diary and let everyone you work with know they won't be able to contact you by email from that date. This will also give you some time to experiment with alternatives in the run-up to your divorce from email.

Look forward to and prepare for the moment you will truly quit. When you are ready, purge your inbox, delete all your emails, disable the email app on your cell phone, and set an 'out-of-email reply,' specifying your new contact details.

Needless to say, if you decide to go cold turkey, you can skip steps 2 and 3, and proceed to step 4 (see page 79).

WQM method II: Eliminating email step by step

This method will let you decide which information to ban from your inbox. Little by little, you will reduce the number of emails you receive. The first steps are relatively easy, such as unsubscribing from newsletters.

After that, you can sink your teeth into the next challenge. I used to receive a lot of emails with to-dos and I would send out many myself. After a few days, I would find myself having to email people for a status update, because I had lost track of the situation. Or I would do a task that someone else had already done, which I didn't know because I hadn't gotten round to reading the email informing me of that. Are you also allocated tasks by email? Log them online or start making (video) calls to quickly discuss actions and tasks. If you then still have questions, you can ask them right away, instead of having to maintain lengthy email conversations.

Do you get a lot of questions by email? You could start a blog to share your knowledge, like IBM's Luis Suarez did. He used a blog to document his inbox zero experiences.

Step 2 (Page 77) will further go into which emails to read and which emails to ignore. Consistent accurate categorization of emails will rapidly reduce the number of emails you have to read.

Step 3 (Page 79) will explain how sending fewer emails will automatically mean you receive fewer emails as well. This can start yielding results very quickly, which is very motivating. It is great to see the volume of emails you receive drop drastically and your inbox reduce to nearly zero emails.

WQM method III: Going on an email diet

You can also quit email by going on an 'email diet.' This is a diet you design yourself.

You decide how long the diet will last (a week, a month), how often you will open your inbox during that period, and how many emails you will be allowed to send. This lets you have your first experiences of life without email without quitting entirely. You can go on such a diet by yourself or with a group, or even as an organization as a whole. The following provides a number of examples of an email diet.

Read your emails at fixed times
A possible first step as part of an email diet is to reduce the number of times a day you check your email to once a day, or even once or twice a week. Reply to emails through social channels to lift the conversation out of your email inbox. This method makes a good stepping stone towards the other WQM methods. These two changes will in themselves already lead to a drastic reduction in email usage.

Go on a thirty-day diet
Over a period of one month, check your email only once a day, and do not send any emails during that period. Reply to incoming emails through social media, by phone, or through personal contact.

Kevin Weijers (civil servant) went on a thirty-day email diet: 'It was an exciting experience to see whether I would be able to rise to the challenge. During my thirty-day email diet, I had to change my bank account number in my payroll details, and one of my colleagues told me that I could really only do that by email. When your salary payments are at stake, it really hits home. I dropped by the payroll department and wrote my account number on a piece of paper and handed it to them with a great big smile on my face. It all worked out in the end!'

It is best to go on an email diet as a group, so that those dieting can exchange experiences and make sure no one falls off the wagon. That is what Tjitske Poelsma and Emmaly Sibbes at Dordrecht's municipal authority did. They set a limit for the number of emails the group members were allowed to send on any given day. 'The weekend before we started the email diet, I worked all out to ensure I could start with a clean slate,' Tjitske Poelsma remembers. 'We had agreed to open our inboxes only once a day, and send no more than three emails a day. For the first few days, not checking my email proved quite difficult. Before I knew it, I'd opened my inbox. It really took some effort to stop doing that, I was hooked.'

I received somewhere between 10,000 to 20,000 emails over the past month — yes, welcome to my regular hell. When I initially said I was quitting for the month, it brought about a few common reactions: 1) 'You're my hero.' 2) 'You're an idiot.' 3) 'It will never work.'

MG SIEGLER, PARTNER AT GOOGLE VENTURES

She continues: 'Aside from enthusiastic reactions, there were also people who said: "But you have to email, it's part of your job, isn't it?" Several staff members thought they would no longer be able to count on me for help: "*I* will suffer the consequences!" but my reply would always be: "I will still do everything you need me to do, just not by email." Older men in particular simply didn't buy that.'

Emmaly: 'We did read our emails. After all, we cannot control how others want to communicate with us, but we can decide what to do with these emails.' It takes time to develop a new way of working. A good idea is to start the day by getting it clear in your head what you want to finish on that day, establish an 'e-mail block' at the end of the day, and set yourself a maximum number of emails you can send, such as three. Sending three emails a day is a good trigger in that it will make you carefully consider whether or not to handle something by email. Without realizing, you will start sharing information in other ways, and use your time and email allowance more efficiently. You are forced to ask yourself: "To whom will I send my three emails?" and: "What is important enough?"'

'You will start selecting accordingly: "I don't have to reply to this, I can deal with this without email, while I do have to respond to this other email,"' says Tjitske. 'In the beginning, I couldn't stick to only three emails a day. I would sneakily send a few more emails at home in the evening. I was basically keeping the emailing going myself. However, by the end of the month, things had improved.'

Both Emmaly and Tjitske felt that their days used to be dictated by email. With nearly sixty emails a day, emailing took up half their time. Cutting that down to a maximum of three emails a day was therefore no mean feat.

And yet, they look back on their month without email with a sense of victory. You do have to come through a kind of detox period, so it takes a while before you get results. It is by no means automatic, you have to really work at it.

Tjitske: 'I think I will take further measures to prevent a relapse. Using alternative communication tools has not yet become second nature, I do sometimes revert to email, but I have every intention to persevere. There have been ups and downs, but my spirits are high!'

When more people join in, it becomes easier. Emmaly: 'Get others to join in! We organized three lunch meetings to explain the options. We showcased the tools on several occasions, which was a huge success. People were curious, everyone had questions about the various options, and was inspired. This had a hugely energizing effect. Whenever people were apprehensive, we would show them there and then how it could work.'
Focus on the people who are excited about it, do not flog dead horses, because that is a waste of energy. When you get your colleagues on board, and make it truly fun for them, everyone will want to give it a go. Quitting email by management directive is futile.

Go on a diet for a week

Does a month without email seem a bit long? A week-long email detox is also an option. A week is just long enough to experience the first benefits, an easy-to-manage time span, and not difficult to explain at work. It's basically a one-week email holiday. Again, you can design the diet based on your own preferences. For it to have a real impact, it would be sensible to stick to a lower limit: open your inbox only once a day and send no more than three emails a day. Do you have the courage to take it to the next level? If so, stop sending emails altogether, and instead reply to emails in other ways, such as by walking over to the sender's desk, picking up the phone, using social media, or inviting the other out to lunch. After this one-week trial period, you can decide to quit email for good, or to try other email detox methods.

Have a fixed weekly no email day
There are also companies that ban email on a specific day every week.[29] In the U.K., Thursdays have been branded No Email Day across the civil service.[30] Stephen Kelly, COO of the Efficiency and Reform Group[31], the ministerial department that ensures the effective running of government, felt overwhelmed by his full inbox every morning. He much prefers informal personal meetings to long emails. Civil servants are encouraged to keep internal emailing to a minimum to make collaboration more efficient.

WQM method IV: Stop gradually
Instead of making a radical break, you can also opt for a less drastic method. When you go for this gradual method, you will, especially in the early days, still use your email. You continue to read incoming emails, but reply to them through social media. And you will stop sending emails, communicating instead through social media, voice and video calls, or simply by stopping by someone's office or having a coffee with someone. This will slowly move the conversation from your inbox to places that are better suited for communication and collaboration. This is how you entice your co-workers to also change their ways of communicating, letting them instantly experience the benefits in practice.

'At one stage, I was spending three hours a day

on email, and I asked myself: "What am I doing?"' says Lucien Engelen of the Radboud REshape Center. He quit gradually. 'I started by only replying to emails through social media, and eventually began to stick to a once-a-week email checking regime. In the end, I stopped using email for business purposes altogether. The great thing is that the subject of "quitting email" has triggered widespread debate at our company. Everybody has an opinion about it. Every time I get on an elevator someone will be talking about quitting email. Some say: "It has really got me thinking about how we work," or the opposite: "Quitting email is not an option here." Some people think you've lost your mind, but luckily I also get a lot of fun out of it. I sometimes think: "Don't you see how strange it actually is that you are so dependent on email?"'

Quitting email is not a goal in itself. Lucien: 'I do still sporadically send an email, to dignitaries, or when there really is no other way because some public organizations can only be reached by email. And there are still people who email me. I try to reply to their emails through alternative channels, such as social networks or by texting them, if only to get them to think about alternatives to email. Sometimes I get responses such as: "OK, but you still read your emails, right?" Some people just don't get it.'

The gradual method may be a very good match with your job or role within your organization. If you are an early adopter, and you enjoy trying out new things, this method is right up your alley. 'I am one of a few at our organization who can do this. I see myself as a kind of jester of the organization, and consider it my job to denounce these kinds of things,' says Lucien. There are also jobs for which you cannot do without email, such as jobs that involve customer contacts. You can then choose to only cut back on internal emails, or stop sending these altogether.

WQM method V: Start small: as a department, team, or project
Is the step of quitting email altogether too great? Try starting small. After all, you can decide how big you want the first step to be. With this method, you agree to quit email as a department, team, or project group. This strategy is one you can implement right away. It is manageable and clearly demarcated, as you know exactly who is involved. Although you are starting small, this method is highly effective, because most email bombs come from your peers within the organization.

It is far easier to start with a small group than to get the entire organization to join in. At the start of a new project, for example, you can decide together to run all project communications through social media.

A journey of a thousand miles begins with a single step.
LAO TZU

Enthusiasts
'The fun thing is that you are embarking on this new initiative with a group of like-minded enthusiasts,' says Linda Westenberg, Communications Advisor at pet product manufacturer

Beaphar. 'We started by using Yammer for an international project, which proved to be more effective than email. It is clear to everyone through which channel we communicate, so no one misses out on anything. The way Yammer is set up makes communication smoother, more natural, and more informal. This, in turn, is what reduces the threshold of getting in touch with each other, as you can use the quick chat feature, and it forges a stronger team spirit. Communication becomes more fun, more personal, and easier. I wouldn't want to go back to email — I don't think I could!'

Marnix Bolkestein, Head of Enforcement, Housing Authority, City of Amsterdam, decided to first trial WQM at his own department. This is a logical first step, because quitting email often clashes with the dominant organizational culture, which has email as its primary communication channel and expects managers to coordinate all information by email. Members of Marnix's staff no longer receive emails from him, but he has not yet managed to fully quit email: 'I do have an email address, because I work in a culture where I have to be reachable by email.'

To Marnix, quitting email is a tool to boost collaboration within his team: 'The ombudsman audited my department in 2010 and concluded that neither internal nor external communications ran smoothly. Social media-based communication and collaboration came as a godsend. I created groups for a number of projects, including one that would be tasked with detecting housing fraud. I invited not only staff to join groups, but also external parties, such as the fire department and housing corporations. It is always fascinating to see how the dynamics of collaboration change. Right from the start, external parties were involved, giving them much better understanding of the choices we made during the process.

Employees have much better insight into each other's activities. In 2012, the ombudsman concluded that enforcement, collaboration, and communication had improved significantly.'

You sometimes have to stress that informal does not equal unprofessional: 'When I open a group, I start out by setting clear standards in terms of content. Every group has a different purpose, and some diversity in messages is fine. But I don't want gossip in the group, I'm very clear on that. We have a departmental group we use to ask each other for

EMAILING GONE TOO FAR.

#WQM

> Dear Willem,
>
> Did you get the report I emailed you yesterday?
>
> Kind regards,
> Famke

> Dear Famke,
>
> Yes. Thank you. I did get the report.
>
> Kind regards,
> Willem

progress updates. When working on a project, participation in a group will add value to the execution of your work.'

Change Driver
Collaboration through social media is not automatic. You need a change driver who regularly posts information on the platform. 'In the beginning, I was posting messages to the group on my own,' Marnix Bolkestein remembers. 'I also consider it part of my job to share relevant information about social issues, such as a report on welfare fraud. We are running a project on the subject, so I posted a link to this report. No matter what level you operate on, it is also good to be aware of debate in society. Group members can decide for themselves what they want to read. In the end, they have to enjoy engaging with the group. Staff initially mainly enjoyed obtaining information from the group. They had to overcome a mental barrier to also start posting messages. One member of our staff recently asked me whether she could post anything. Needless to say, she does not need my permission for that.'

It is also a matter of being patient. In the beginning, the group needs to invest some time in becoming familiar with the technology involved in online collaboration before it starts yielding results. In some cases, employees do not immediately see the benefits, and therefore don't want to go along with it. Marnix: 'Every time I launch a new project, there are one or two who don't want to join in. I've noticed that these employees have to overcome a kind of anxiety before they are ready to join our online platform. That requires perseverance and not being fazed by anything. Eventually, they sign up anyway and experience the benefits for themselves. The great thing is that everyone increasingly becomes involved. My staff members now say Yammer is better than email. I draw my conviction that this works from the projects I do and the results we are achieving. More and more people have made the step, which motivates me enormously.'

It is a good idea to create a closed group for certain departments or projects and invite only direct stake-holders. Broad input on your idea may be very valuable, but some people think they always have to express an opinion.

Works council
For a works council, social media offer an ideal opportunity of getting staff involved. 'We have meanwhile accumulated a number of successful examples,' says Jan Kuijk, secretary of the City of Amsterdam's Works Council. 'It is easy to involve employees in the decision-making process when you can run specific subjects by them. Especially when there were organizational changes at stake, such as the implementation of flexible working hours, this worked very well. Using open groups ensured that far more people than before were involved, with employees immediately responding to proposals. They also shared experiences and gave each other tips. We got very good results.'

This also ended up changing the way the council operated: 'We, as the works council, were enabled to use the information we obtained much more strategically. We used to first collect people's comments, and only at the end of the process collate the action points into our advice. Now the relevant departments immediately take up the action points. This enables you to jointly head in the same direction.'

It's not about being right, it's about triggering a new story.

DAAN ROOSEGAARDE, ARTIST AND INNOVATOR

Occasionally, the council does still use email. 'It is something you have to keep working at,' says Jan Kuijk. 'Sometimes I feel like Don Quixote. Especially when I get emails asking "Who has an answer to this?" followed by people sending their replies to the whole group. I am really not interested in reading sixty persons' answers to one question.

That's when an online group is so much more convenient. I sometimes wonder why it is so hard to get people to join in. I just cannot explain that stubbornness. Some of my colleagues even brag about their email inbox being jam-packed.

Let's stop that once and for all! The old way of working is often completely devoid of all creativity. I can see the benefits of online collaboration and regularly use brief instructions to show others how it works. Where email is static, online is dynamic, and you have to learn to harness that. I feel like I'm waging a kind of war, because you need active participation to get new media off the ground. Technologically, it's all possible, but humans are slow to catch on. It's the future, and you will change eventually.'

Don't become a missionary trying to persuade everyone to join you in quitting email. Besides positive responses and understanding, you will also come up against resistance. Make it clear why you are taking this step and share your experiences. Why is this working for you, what does this new way of working give you in concrete terms? This is how you will eventually achieve the most.

Develop your own WQM method
There is, of course, nothing that stops you from developing your own We Quit eMail method. I am very curious to hear about your approach and invite you to share it on wequitmail.com, so that others can benefit from your experiences.

Exit
You have selected a We Quit eMail strategy and know how you will go about eliminating email from your life. Let everyone know which method you have chosen and as of when you will be quitting or cutting back.

Step 2: scan your inbox

If you have selected the first method in step 1, you can immediately proceed to step 4, and skip this step and the next one. Chances are, however, that you went for one of the other strategies. If so, this second step and the third step may help you in significantly reducing the volume of emails in your inbox.

Take a critical look at the information you are receiving by email. Do tasks, questions, newsletters, or social media notifications dominate? Merely looking at your emails in this way for a few days will quickly reveal a pattern. Make categories to classify the information. Below you will find a number of possible categories.

Emails you basically never read
- ☐ Newsletters
- ☐ Advertising
- ☐ Surveys
- ☐ Social media notifications
- ☐ Links to news items

Work-related emails
- ☐ Updates
- ☐ Questions
- ☐ Tasks and actions
- ☐ Documents
- ☐ Appointment requests and confirmations
- ☐ Conversations through the Subject field that are a lot like chat sessions

Emails you would prefer not to receive
- ☐ Emails containing only one word ('OK' or 'agreed')
- ☐ Out-of-office replies
- ☐ CCs and BCCs
- ☐ Emails for information purposes
- ☐ Emails to a large group of people
- ☐ Emails to the entire organization
- ☐ Emails you sent to yourself: as a reminder, articles you want to keep, etc

Classify the emails into the categories you have selected. Next, decide which emails you will first start banning from your inbox, such as those from the 'Emails you basically never read' category. The first thing I did was to unsubscribe from all the newsletters I was receiving, and then mark all advertising email as spam, disable social media notifications, and ask co-workers not to share links to interesting articles by email. This first step alone already brought significant relief. As soon as you are ready to take it further, move on the next category. What I did was to keep tasks and actions out of my inbox. By moving these to an online platform, I seriously cut down the number of emails I received.

Exit

You now know what kind of information is clogging up your inbox. And you have taken the first measures to receive fewer emails.

Step 3: send fewer emails

It may sound like stating the obvious, but to me it was a real eye-opener. It is undeniable: the more emails you send, the more you receive. Every email I sent would easily produce ten replies. The easiest route toward an empty inbox is to only send emails that are absolutely necessary.

Carefully consider whether a reply is really required. A percentage of the emails you receive are unnecessary, and so are an even greater percentage of your replies. Don't feel guilty about not replying.[32] *When you take a more conscious approach to email, you will find that many things will not have to be handled (by email). Be creative!*

Exit
You are now sending fewer emails, and consequently seeing the number of replies in your inbox diminish.

Step 4: make new work arrangements

The way you communicate and collaborate changes as soon as you throw email overboard. This affects not only you, but everyone around you. It is therefore advisable to make new work arrangements based on what you want to achieve together. Use the results of step 2 to discuss information

needs with your co-workers and other peers, and
agree on how to go about it.

---

*Do not scrap the old way of working by introducing
six new tools at once. This is far too overwhelming
for most people. Besides, you cannot change your
behavior and way of working in one single action, it
requires time. Begin with one or two crucial tools. As
soon as these have taken root, gradually start using
more tools.*

The following questions are possible guiding
principles in making arrangements that work for
your team or organization. Bear in mind that it is
always a good idea to elect a change driver or single
point of contact, in other words someone people
can turn to with their questions or doubts. In
practice, you will see that the team soon picks up
the habit of calling each other to account on errors
and asking each other for help. They become
self-regulating.

What information to share

What kind of information should we post on the
online platform? It needs to be clear to everyone
that the platform is not a kind of chat room, but a
place for work-related communication. You could
set the following rules:
- Everyone must post a weekly work update.
- Post only work-related information.
- Use the platform to submit agenda items for
  the next meeting. When no one submits

agenda items, the meeting is automatically
canceled.
- Do not use the group to share links to videos
  and articles. Do that elsewhere.
- Do not share personal matters. We will be
  opening a separate 'advice column group' for
  the entire organization for that.
- Do not reply to messages using only 'OK,'
  'agreed,' or 'thanks' but use the thumb-up
  emoticon instead.

What to discuss online and what to discuss in a meeting

Online platforms help co-workers stay in touch in
between scheduled meetings, changing the
purpose of in-person meetings. Agree on what to
share on the online platform and what to discuss
at in-person meetings. For example:
- Information we need to do our job must be
  shared online.
- In-person meetings are social occasions that
  allow us to look each other in the eye and ask
  how things are going. At these meetings, we
  will share knowledge, brainstorm to trigger
  ideas, inspire each other by sharing best
  practices, and discuss real-life cases.
- At meetings, we will discuss upcoming
  milestones, agree on who will do what and
  when, while subsequently sharing progress on
  the online platform.
- Post weekly progress updates online. That
  means we will no longer have to ask everyone
  at the meeting what they have done, because
  we already know, which will make meetings far
  less tedious.

- ☐ At meetings, we will not discuss minutes from the previous meeting. Minutes (if you decide to take them) and actions are posted online, and also discussed online. It is everyone's personal responsibility to update their list of actions for the next meeting.
- ☐ Discuss which subjects you would prefer to share online and which ones face to face. This will eliminate the need for questions before closure, as well as notices, at meetings. Documents and feedback are posted in the online group, unless it concerns something you want to share privately.
- ☐ Whenever interim verbal consultations are required, we use video conferencing.

How often to check online

Agree with each other how often you want team members to log on. My experience is that once a week is enough for most projects, provided everyone knows when they are supposed to have things finished. In the case of teams that have to share large volumes of work-related information, checking in once a day is often the minimum.

This is a very important arrangement to make! When you agree to check in only once a week, employees will really regain control of their work. You will avoid team members responding to every single notification, which only makes everyone involved restless.

Obtain or provide?

This new way of working comes with a responsibility shift, as employees are no longer obliged to provide information, but instead to obtain information. As a professional, you are responsible for staying informed. You can no longer hide behind excuses such as: 'You didn't CC me' or: 'I didn't know that.'

What practical arrangements to make

Make practical arrangements about the use of tools (refer to the list of available tools in this chapter). Have employees use the subject line to specify the name of the person from whom they at least need a reply. This makes it easy to scan the messages for the ones that are actually relevant for you, and only open those ones.

What is our emergency channel?

Agree on how to get in touch with each other in case of urgent matters. Whenever something needs urgent attention, I often see people fall back on email, because they are afraid their message will otherwise not be read in time. You could, however, use WhatsApp or Telegram for this purpose. I have found that such an emergency channel is rarely used, because you generally get your answer quickly enough on the platform.

How to handle discipline: doing both is more time-consuming

Explicitly agree with everyone to quit email. If you keep using email alongside the online platform, you will be wasting a lot of time. Besides, it soon becomes unmanageable, as you lose sight of where to find the information you need.

Appoint a team member who will keep all other members on their toes. Quitting email means changing your current way of working. As soon as things get hectic, people are very likely to relapse into their old ways. Whenever that happens, it helps to have one team member to ask the relapsing team member to post the information online as well.

How would you prefer to work?

Discuss with each other what the ideal day at work is like for you. Collaboration will improve when you know each other's preferences in terms of working hours and contact channels, as well as needs for personal contact. Team members can work different schedules, as long as there are opportunities for collaboration. One size does not fit all.

As a professional, you are responsible for staying informed.

I, for one, enjoy working in the evenings, and I don't like unannounced phone calls, because they interfere with what I am doing at that moment. A colleague of mine, on the other hand, prefers to work nine to five, and does not mind being called out of the blue. As long as we keep each other's preferences in mind and work together well, all is well. When we have to hit a deadline on Friday, it doesn't matter if I do my bit during the daytime or in the evening, as long as I have it done on time. What I like about having my colleagues' preferences out in the open like this is that it makes you see there are ways of working that differ from yours. Gone are the days of a manager emailing the entire department in the evening and coming in to the office at 8.30 the next morning assuming everyone has read the email.

What are digital skills like at your organization?
Discuss your digital skills and those of the people you work with. Make sure everyone is able to join in. Consider using the following ways of getting staff skilled up.

Organize workshops
Give presentations and workshops on using tools that are aimed at reducing email usage and facilitating collaboration. Walk colleagues through the process of creating an account, installing an app on a device, using the various buttons, and show them how to use the platform as part of their day to day activities.

I have found that people are willing, but hesitant to independently familiarize themselves with new tools. Your explanation should not solely focus on how a tool works, but also on why it is exciting to share a draft version of a document with colleagues and allow them a sneak peek of what you are doing.

Organize train-the-trainer workshops
One particularly effective method is to train a group of internal staff members in online collaboration and communication to enable them to subsequently train their co-workers. One-on-one sessions work well for managers, setting them on their way toward smarter collaboration.

Organize regular ToolTime meetings
ToolTime meetings not only allow staff to ask questions about tools, they also provide an opportunity for colleagues to share experiences, tips, tricks, and handy apps.

By having these kinds of brief meetings, you are enabling your staff members to help each other make progress. There is often more expertise available across the company than you think. You can, of course, tap into that expertise by setting up a 'Help' group. Especially for a team with less developed digital skills, it is always comforting to have something to fall back on.

Put smarter collaboration on the agenda
When embarking on the We Quit eMail journey, it is advisable to make smarter collaboration a monthly fixture on the agenda. Discuss progress, what employees like about it, but also possible problems that arise. Computer illiterates will be

quick to say 'See, it doesn't work!' at the slightest setback. They may be unable to find the delete button to delete a post, or lack the confidence to ask for help, and subsequently refuse to use the tool altogether. Whenever that happens, the best thing to do is to show them how to do it and discuss their experiences to get them back on board. It's like riding a bike: when you fall off, you just have to get back on and keep going. What has struck me is that the ones who initially show most resistance often end up becoming your fiercest ambassadors.

Pay extra attention to special groups
One example of a special group is the secretarial office. This department often plays a pivotal role in internal collaboration and communication. By getting these employees to sign up to the new way of working, you will significantly speed up reduction of email usage. Them becoming online collaboration ambassadors will propel the entire organization toward online collaboration. If you don't manage to get them to join you, there is likely to be little change, as they keep emailing documents, requesting agenda items by email, and otherwise communicating by email. The same goes for managers. When you teach them to send fewer emails, the total number of emails sent across the organization will automatically drop drastically. You can train them and give them tips on how to send fewer emails by setting them an email limit, prohibiting email forwarding, or only allowing it in an emergency, as well as including fewer recipients, and helping them choose a different communica-

tion channel. Give them weekly feedback to improve their strategy.

Exit
You have now discussed information needs with your co-workers and agreed on a new way of working, tools, and how to use them to maximize efficiency.

Step 5: choose your tools

Having completed step 4, you are now aware of how and with whom you communicate. The next step is to assess what information you really need to be able to do your job well. Needless to say, this will differ from one job to the next. We will therefore start this step by matching the various online tools to different types of jobs. Following that, we will list the most important tools, categorized based on the tasks for which they are best suited.

Do not limit yourself to one tool that is supposed to do everything, but make a selection of tools that best support your work (see overview on page 96). The total offering is like a toolbox, from which you pick the tools you need for a specific task. After all, a carpenter will not use a screwdriver to hammer a nail into the wall.

Privacy

Before you start using a tool, consider what kind of information you will be sharing through it, and think about security. Many organizations will, for example, buy a license for an online platform or store confidential data on secure servers. What is the responsible approach to storing information in the cloud? This is a question everyone needs to answer, not only people who are quitting email.

It is highly advisable to distinguish between information you share freely, information you can store in the cloud, and information for which you need to log on to a secure system. Do bear in mind that this is not always your data. When you work for the government, for example, you are dealing with citizens' data, which you must handle responsibly.

Raise awareness of this discussion across the organization in a fun way. How do you use certain business information at a certain location, on a certain device, and with a certain tool? What are the risks, and how can you handle them? It is ultimately about individual employees' awareness and sense of responsibility.

Which tools suit your job?

Which collaboration tools are best suited to your activities? The following provides a number of examples. Not all will apply to you, but it may just give you ideas.

Flexible employee

Imagine you collect a lot of information for your work, such as articles, tweets, and photos. Every time you encounter relevant information, you send it to your own email account. You also talk to a lot of people at work, and make notes of the things you discuss. Now and again, you suddenly think of things you still have to do. You also work with co-workers on short-term projects, such as a magazine. The question is how to rearrange your work to be able to do it without using email.

To gather information and take notes during meetings, I use an online notepad: Evernote. The advantage of this application is that you store everything in one place, making it easy to find information when you need it. You can also record action points here, or put them on an online to-do list.

When working on something like a magazine, you can select a tool that allows several people to work on one document at the same time, such as Google Drive. To exchange information, you can use a collaboration platform, such as Yammer.

For visual material (which you will need in your magazine), you can use Pinterest. On Pinterest, you can pin photos you like, fun quotes, links to YouTube videos, etc. to a single board. Other photo sharing options include Dropbox, Flickr, or a folder on Google Drive.

Self-employed

As a self-employed professional, you often work for multiple clients and in different places. Your work may include collaboration with various peers on a project, writing plans, giving presentations, and training people. Apart from that, you compile offers and send invoices. You meet a lot of new people all the time, who all give you their business cards.

Working on projects together is something you can do through social media tools such as Yammer, Facebook, Podio, and Asana. When you need to work on a document together, Google Drive is a good option. Prezi or Haiku Deck are tools for the design and creation of presentations. There are several possible ways of making offers and invoices. Google Drive is a free option. Personally, I use Offorte (for a fee) to make offers, and MoneyBird (for a fee) for invoices. I submit my offers and invoices to my clients through social media. What you can do with the business cards you get is to take a picture of them and save them in Evernote. I don't use business cards myself, but instead immediately add contacts on LinkedIn.

Manager

As a manager, you take part in different kinds of meetings and are responsible for running large teams of employees and managing external parties. You communicate a lot, read a lot of articles, write plans, give presentations, and keep a log of your actions. You receive a lot of emails from employees asking you to weigh in, and need to be able to monitor operations.

For quick communications in between tasks, you can make phone calls, text, or use WhatsApp or Telegram. Internal communications can be handled through Yammer, which lets you reach all staff members with one message. You can also create closed groups for consultations with management board members and staff, so you can give feedback and track progress. The iBabs app will ensure you stay on top of your meeting schedule, store all documents you need for specific appointments in one place, and also lets you make notes. And you can use your cell phone to track your actions, using the Reminders app, for example.

Field staff
As a field staff member, you are barely at the office, but instead on the road a lot or visiting clients.

To be able to quickly get in touch with the office, for example when your plans change, WhatsApp or Telegram are ideal tools. You can also use them to ask co-workers for advice and share photos. A platform such as Yammer lets you stay in touch with the entire organization, while also making it easy to swap shifts. Internal platforms also allow

Using online tools is not a goal in itself.

you to make direct changes to systems. Platforms can also be used to maintain customer contacts. I use Facebook to send pictures to my car mechanic and ask for advice.

When you need to make a note of something, you can grab your cell and make a note in Evernote, so you can retrieve it anytime and anywhere. (Video) calls are a way of quickly taking stock of a situation or handling consultations remotely.

Volunteer

When you work as a volunteer, on the board of a club for example, you will be sent a lot of information by email ahead of meetings or just to keep you informed. This is also an environment that is susceptible to email bombs, with everyone individually replying to one email.

Select an online platform on which you can share news and documents and discuss things with each other. This will make it easy to stay in touch in between meetings.

Management Assistant

As a management assistant, you are a true linchpin. You answer the phone, schedule appointments, prepare documents, record actions, and arrange all sorts of other things in between.

I, myself, share a to-do list with my assistant in Trello. I put tasks on the lists and she sends feedback on what has been done about it, or creates a task for me. This ensures that you can both easily stay on top of things. The telephone switchboard texts me whenever there was a call for me. For assistants, texting, WhatsApp, and Telegram are ideal for making last-minute arrangements. You can post documents to special meeting apps, such as iBabs, or save them to online folders on Dropbox or Google Drive. Lists are easy to maintain in Google Forms, where all information is received in one place.

Teacher

As a teacher, you do a lot of communicating with fellow teachers, colleagues, students, and possibly also parents. You make presentations and share knowledge.

At school, an internal system or Facebook can be used to share information about, for example, classroom changes within a private group. You can also use such a platform for discussions or to answer questions. Twitter is a good tool for communication with colleagues, while Scoop.it lets you share interesting articles. Keeping a blog on Tumblr is a fine way of sharing knowledge, while you can also use this medium to share lesson materials. You can use Skype and Google Hangouts alongside your in-person lessons to tutor students.

At elementary schools, private Facebook groups are already being used successfully, replacing written notes to parents. Schools can share what pupils have been learning, and use their Facebook group to advertise for volunteers. Parents can also contact each other through this medium.

Begin by defining your goal

No matter what your job entails, you should always begin by defining your goal: why are you doing this and what do you want to achieve? Like I said, using online tools is not an aim in itself. Consider which tool is best for each communication need. Choose the channels that work best for you.

The crux of quitting email lies more in your mindset than in the tools. As soon as you have made the switch mentally, choosing the appropriate tools will be a relatively easy next step. There are hundreds of tools available to help you work smarter. What you choose depends heavily on your personal preferences. The fastest way of finding out which tools best suit you is to experiment.

Below you will find a number of tools that have helped me be more efficient in my work and enabled me to do more in less time. This list is by no means exhaustive, but it will set you on your way in choosing your tools. Don't let the large number put you off. Simply select one or two to start with. You will soon see that a number of these tools do exactly the same thing.

The previous section may have already given you an idea of which tools would be suitable for you. But perhaps your head is spinning with all those names of different online possibilities. The following list provides an overview of today's most commonly used tools.

Tools

This is a list of the tools that are currently the most commonly used.

Online collaboration

- Yammer
- Facebook
- Google+
- Asana
- Podio
- Teamwork
- Huddle

Online conferencing

- Skype
- Google Hangouts
- FaceTime
- Lync
- FaceTalk

Online business networking

- LinkedIn
- Quora
- Plaxo
- Viadeo
- Xing

Taking notes

- Evernote
- Notes

Managing to-do lists

- Trello
- Wunderlist
- Basecamp
- Reminders
- Nozbe

Making presentations and mind maps

- Prezi
- Haiku Deck
- Mindmeister

Collaborative file editing

- Google Drive
- OneDrive
- Yammer
- Basecamp
- Hackpad
- iCloud

File sharing

- Google Drive
- Dropbox
- OneDrive
- Box
- Sharepoint
- Yammer
- iCloud
- iBabs
- Scribd
- Issuu

Instant messaging

- Skype
- Facebook Messenger
- Google Hangouts
- WhatsApp
- Telegram
- WeChat
- iMessage

Update sharing and tracking

- Flipboard
- HootSuite
- Scoop.it
- IFTTT

Social networks

- Twitter
- Facebook
- Path

Blogging

- Tumblr
- WordPress

Visual communication

- Snapchat
- Vine
- Instagram
- Pinterest
- ooVoo

Video

- YouTube
- Vimeo
- PowToon
- Animoto

Graphic communication

- Piktochart
- Infogr.am
- ComicLife

Social media is by no means a panacea. You have to invest some time before you can actually start reaping the benefits. Try out online tools and gradually start using them more and more. Changing your behavior will inevitably take time, as will getting used to a tool.

You could consider going on a voyage of discovery in the world of tools, looking for resources for smarter working methods. Emmaly Sibbes: 'What I really liked was picking out all the new tools, I loved it! I'd always been interested in these kinds of things, and We Quit eMail gave me the opportunity to find out more about them. I didn't focus so much on the tools, but predominantly on what I could get out of them in my work.'

People often say to me: 'I also want to cut back on my emailing, tell me what tool I should use.' Unfortunately, that's not how it works. Sibbes: 'I don't mind working through multiple channels. I have one device on which I can check all these channels, and you can configure them the way you want. I like having several channels, each with its own special purpose. I use each of my channels for one thing only. Channels also change more quickly, which is something I like and find interesting. I'm somewhat older, and I notice that I'm reluctant to switch to other channels, but I do think it is best to keep abreast of these things. If I'm not careful, I'll become a fossil! I don't want that to happen. I hope IT will provide us with more ways of keeping up with these changes. It requires a different perspective on information management and automation at organizations.'

What marks the online tools discussed here is

that each and every one of them is very good at one thing. Which tool to use will therefore differ per situation. You can, for example, use Twitter to keep up with the news, share knowledge, and build a network, but when you need to work on a document with someone, Google Drive is the more obvious choice. Organizations that go for only one tool often see implementation fail, as single tools have to be able to do everything and therefore end up being complex systems. So choose the tools to match your activities, and link these to the tools that those people you communicate with are already using. Find it difficult to choose? Choose the tools your network is already using. 'I'm on the platforms where my network is,' says Lucien Engelen. 'At my department, we use Yammer to communicate and Wunderlist for tasks. Other than that, I'm on Twitter, Facebook, and LinkedIn.'

Online collaboration
- ☐ Yammer
- ☐ Facebook
- ☐ Google+
- ☐ Asana
- ☐ Podio
- ☐ Teamwork
- ☐ Huddle

Using the above social platforms, you can create a place where everyone from across the organization can share knowledge and collaborate. Some are used for project communication, such as Facebook and Google+, while others, such as Podio and Asana, are better suited for project management.

One online platform that is widely used at companies is Yammer, which is a kind of internal Facebook for knowledge sharing, asking questions, and group collaboration. This is a medium that fosters cross-border collaboration (across physical national borders, but also across hierarchical ones), because it makes it easy for people to find and get in touch with each other. Yammer is also elbowing out the intranet, as it facilitates information sharing across an entire company and can quickly get interaction going. Departments and teams will generally have a private group on an online platform for day-to-day communications, document sharing, and tasks. And you can also chat with co-workers whenever they are online. Collaborating with people outside the company is possible through an external network. Yammer is a web-based tool you can install on your computer as a program, or as an app on your tablet or smartphone.

Facebook Groups lets you work and communicate with groups of people in a private virtual space. Group members can respond to each other's messages, chat, upload pictures and documents, create events, and work on documents together.

Google+ lets you work together in a community, keeping your fellow community members up to date and sharing pictures, videos, and links.[33] You can join communities whose interests you share, but you can also start your own community. A key advantage of Google+ is that its Hangouts feature offers video conferencing. Some people claim that the ample range of Google+ features is heralding the end of email.[34]

In terms of the features they offer, Yammer, Facebook and Google+ are fairly similar. I always choose based on which platform the people I work with use. Increasing numbers of companies are choosing to set up, for reasons relating to privacy, their own network for online collaboration and communication.

Asana caters to project management by bringing conversations and tasks together in one place. Podio is a combined social, project management, marketing, and sales platform. You get real-time updates on progress, leads and sales, as well as notifications of when employees have scheduled their vacation. Patrick Mulder: 'For our tourist offices, we have switched project communications to Podio. All information relating to a particular project goes through this platform, on desktop PCs, iPads, and iPhones, making all information available to everyone, even to external project team members.' There are also alternative tools, such as Teamwork and Huddle.[35]

Online conferencing
- ☐ Skype
- ☐ Google Hangouts
- ☐ FaceTime
- ☐ Lync
- ☐ FaceTalk

Online conferencing through Skype, FaceTime, Google Hangouts, or Lync is extremely effective.

What is striking is that employees often use these tools in their private lives to stay in touch with friends and family abroad, but rarely use them for business purposes. Connecting with people through Skype or Google Hangouts will eliminate travel and is particularly convenient when you want to quickly catch up with people, discuss things, or work together on something for an afternoon. In the latter case, all you would need to do is open a document or presentation and work on it with several people at a time, while talking to each other on Skype or another video conferencing platform.

Skype and FaceTime (Apple) are used for one-on-one meetings. Lync and Google Hangouts are particularly suited for group meetings. What I like about Skype is that it allows you to send instant messages and share files during the meeting. Skype's group video conferencing options are limited, offering only audio and no video, unless you sign up for a paid account. A good alternative is Google Hangouts, which does offer free group video conferencing. Integration with Google Drive lets you work on a document while you are in a video conference, which is very handy indeed.

Google also has an additional service called Google Helpouts, which gives you (free or paid) access to professional help in different areas. Lync is a for-a-fee tool that companies use for instant messaging, video calls, and online conferencing. At the Radboud University Medical Center, they use FaceTalk for video calls with patients and care providers worldwide over a secure Internet connection.

Online business networking
- ☐ LinkedIn
- ☐ Quora
- ☐ Plaxo
- ☐ Viadeo
- ☐ Xing

Instead of exchanging business cards, I use LinkedIn to add people I meet to my network. LinkedIn is a profile website where people post their resumé and where you can directly exchange business contact details. It is also a useful resource when searching for job vacancies. LinkedIn is like an online business card organizer, one that enables you to quickly find people.

The great thing about LinkedIn is that your peers will ensure their contact details remain up to date, whereas details on a business card are often outdated. Building an online network on LinkedIn gives you easy access to business contacts when you need them. It is also handy when you need someone with certain skills or want to get in contact with someone you only know indirectly.

Forbes has already named LinkedIn the best network for professionals of our time.[36] Alternative networks you can use to display your knowledge include Quora. This question-and-answer website lets users showcase their expertise. There are three further networks that are used as alternatives to LinkedIn, namely Plaxo, the largest online address book, Viadeo, which is particularly popular in France, India, and China, and Xing, which is enjoying great success in Germany.

Making notes
☐ Evernote
☐ Notes

Making notes online has proven to be an absolute godsend for me. Whenever I used to jot a note down on a piece of paper, I would never have it on me when I needed it, or I could no longer decipher my own handwriting. Given that I now write my notes online in Evernote, I always have them on hand. Evernote is my digital memory.

Evernote is a digital notepad. I use it to save documents, notes, links, pictures, and sound recordings. Have a brilliant idea? Save it immediately, so you can retrieve that brainwave later. Like that wine? Take a picture of the label and save it in Evernote. You can also use it to set reminders and manage your to-do lists. Evernote offers a search feature that allows you to find specific notes and documents in no time. Evernote works on all devices. Especially for people whose inbox has morphed into a kind of archive, Evernote is a real must-have! Sibbes: 'I was already using Evernote, but when I quit email, I suddenly discovered that it could do a lot more. Evernote is now my personal external hard drive. It can take any kind of information, and everything is easy to find. You can search by title, keyword, location, or tag. Notes on paper simply do not offer that kind of findability. It is nice not to have to keep useless information up to date anymore.'

Personally, I also use the standard Notes app that comes preinstalled on Apple devices to make a

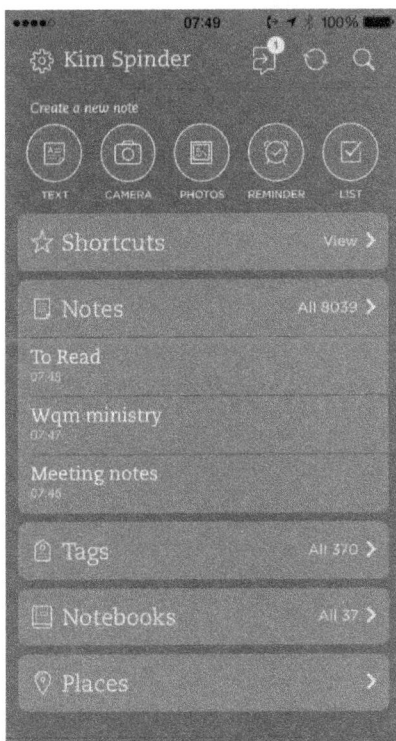

quick note of something or to save notes that I
want to always have on hand, both online and
offline. You can also sync these notes to be able to
access them from other devices.

Managing to-do lists
- [ ] Trello
- [ ] Wunderlist
- [ ] Basecamp
- [ ] Reminders
- [ ] Nozbe

Many people use their inbox as a kind of to-do list,
but a designated online task list works much
better. Whenever you spontaneously think of
something you need to do, you can instantly add
that task to your list, keeping all your to-dos
together on one convenient list that you can access
anytime and anywhere. There are numerous to-do
apps available. Which one you choose depends on

New features Sign out

Basecamp Projects Calendar **Everything** Progress Everyone Me

🔍 Jump to a project, person, label, or search...

Here's a collection of everything from all your projects.

Browse every discussion

Review all open to-dos

See every single file

Read all text documents

Show all forwarded emails

your personal preferences. When you only need to be able to record tasks for yourself, Evernote is a good option. I use Trello (free) and Basecamp (paid) to keep track of tasks involving several people. Trello is comparable to a planning board that is filled with post-its with tasks written on them. You can track what you are working on and the progress you are making. Basecamp lets you specify for each task who is working on it and when it must be completed, as well as include relevant documents. I always make a task list at the start, giving everyone involved at-a-glance insight into the state of affairs. Whenever you think of a task, you can add it to the list immediately.

I use the Reminders app on my phone for personal reminders. Alternative reminder applications are Nozbe and Wunderlist. The latter lets you create group task lists.

Making presentations and mind maps
- ☐ Prezi
- ☐ Haiku Deck
- ☐ MindMeister

For presentations, mind maps, or schedules, I prefer to use online visual tools, such as Prezi, Haiku Deck, or MindMeister. Instead of endlessly sending presentation files back and forth, asking for input from colleagues, my fellow team members and I work together on a central presentation or visualization at the same time. Prezi is the tool we most often use for that. Prezi lets you add images, text, and videos to a large canvas. And you then decide on a sequence for your presentation by creating a path. You can zoom in on key components of the presentation and easily return to the overall view, making your presentation more dynamic. MindMeister is the solution we use to, for example, create a mind map and jointly make an outline of a project, or for the initial brainstorm session on a particular subject. All team members can post their ideas on this platform simultaneously.

When you need a visual presentation to pitch a proposal or present a progress report, Haiku Deck is a great option. What is particularly useful about this tool is that it lets you search and use royalty-free images directly from the tool. This has saved me a lot of time, as non-copyrighted images are always hard to find. And you can include notes with additional information or insert a link to Google Drive, where you and your team can continue your collaboration. This also makes this

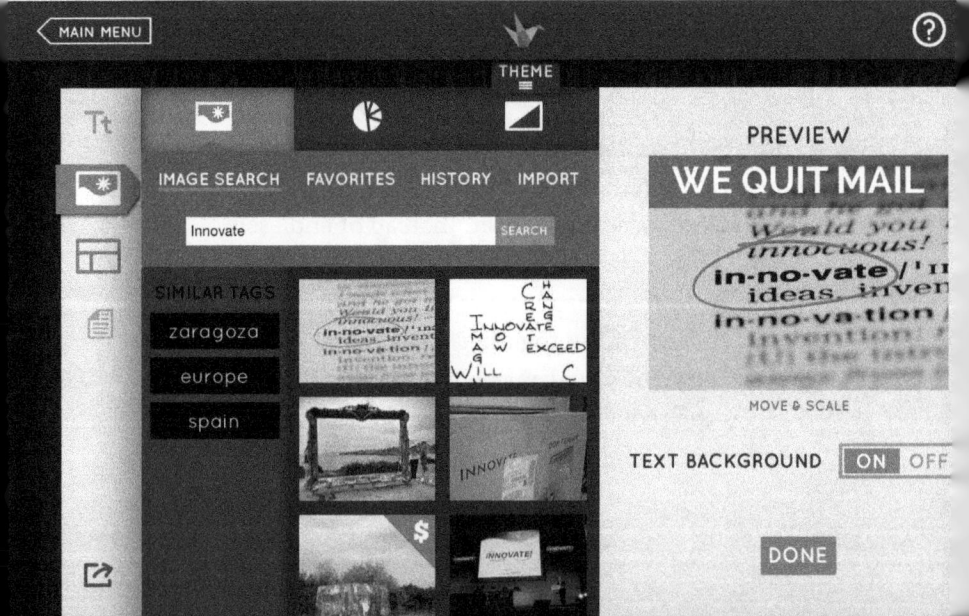

tool an extremely handy classroom resource. Haiku Deck forces you to keep your presentation visual, and use only headlines instead of larger blocks of text. This tool is best used individually.

File sharing

- ☐ Google Drive
- ☐ Dropbox
- ☐ OneDrive
- ☐ Box
- ☐ SharePoint
- ☐ Yammer
- ☐ iCloud
- ☐ iBabs
- ☐ Scribd
- ☐ Issuu

When working in a group, it is convenient to have a joint platform for documents, photos, logos, and other content. You will then have all relevant documents in one folder and accessible to everyone. Dropbox is a popular online storage service that facilitates online file and image storage and sharing. I use Dropbox to share photos or as an archive during projects. Google Drive, OneDrive, Box, and SharePoint all offer the option of enabling folders for file sharing and are great when you're working in teams. Collaboration platforms such as Yammer offer a comment option as well as file sharing.

Apple has its own online storage service, iCloud. iCloud does not lend itself to teamwork, but you can use it to store your presentations, documents, or photos.

Have a lot of meetings involving confidential documents? If so, a special app such as iBabs (paid) offers an easy way to securely share documents and go paperless. You will then have all documents conveniently arranged in your diary, while you can add comments to them directly. For documents you want to publish online, you can use Scribd or Issuu.

Collaborative file editing

- ☐ Google Drive
- ☐ OneDrive
- ☐ Yammer
- ☐ Basecamp
- ☐ Hackpad
- ☐ iCloud

It is ideal to be able to work on a file with several people at the same time, and in real time. Contrary to sending a file back and forth by email, using a service such as Google Drive will not lead to multiple versions of the document. And you won't have everyone running a spell check anymore. Aside from that, you can see each other's feedback

Google

Search Drive

Drive   My Drive > **We Quit Mail** ▾

NEW

My Drive
Incoming
Recent
Starred
Bin

Wqm English.pdf

WQM Book

Tools WQM

spread wqm

and won't have to process each comment separately, as they all appear in the same place. Everyone can work on the document at the same time, see what others have done, and enter comments immediately. You can also share folders holding multiple documents.

I also use Google Drive during my English class, as a live and interactive whiteboard on which we work together on exercises during and after class. It is an ideal tool, as it provides a very effective way of accurately tracking progress. 'No more email searches, no more lost files, and no more days spent digging through my inbox,' says Carolyn Nelson, my English teacher. 'I started using Google Drive with Kim, and I'm now using it for collaborations with people across the globe.'

You can also use Google Drive on your own to save you from having to email files to yourself by instead creating them online, so you can access them anytime and anywhere.

Yammer and Basecamp also offer a notes feature that enables collaborative document editing. When working in a group, it is, for example, helpful to take minutes and record tasks. However, for larger documents, I always switch to Google Drive. Want an alternative? OneDrive lets you share pictures and files, simultaneously work on them with others, and create and share folders. Hackpad and iCloud make it very easy to work on a document with several people at the same time.

Instant messaging
- ☐ Skype
- ☐ Facebook Messenger

- ☐ Google Hangouts
- ☐ WhatsApp
- ☐ Telegram
- ☐ WeChat
- ☐ iMessage

For every message I need to send, I assess which channel will be most efficient. I also factor in urgency. People often don't need your message as urgently as you initially think. For pressing or even urgent matters, I use WhatsApp or Telegram. These messaging platforms have emerged as a popular alternative to texting, because you don't have to pay to send a message. Besides sending messages, these platforms also let you create groups and send images, videos, and voice recordings to your contacts.

I use WhatsApp and Telegram for quick communications and to make arrangements with people, both individually and in groups. When creating a group, you should agree with your fellow group members to only use the group for a specific purpose, as it will otherwise soon get 'cluttered' with all kinds of messages. If a group is intended for business purposes only, you could consider also creating a second group alongside it for non-work-related matters.

WeChat is an alternative to WhatsApp and Telegram.

For project communications, we often use Facebook Messenger, for which you don't have to open Facebook. Messenger is a stand-alone instant messaging program that shows you who is online and when your message was read. You can send messages to a group or individual, and also share photos and stickers, and make free phone calls. I use this service a lot with people with whom I have to collaborate intensively during a project, or as a deadline nears, because it allows us to consult and make decisions quickly.

Skype is a very handy tool for quick chat sessions and file sharing. Google's Hangouts app also has an instant messaging feature which, besides video calls, lets you share messages, photos, and emoticons, both one on one and in a group. You can see whether or not messages have been read and who is available. There is also a feature you can set to notify you whenever someone comes back online.

If yours is an Apple device, you can use iMessage for free messaging and video, picture, and contact sharing. When sending a message to someone who does not have iMessage on their device, this tool will automatically switch to texting. What is particularly useful about this tool is that it doesn't matter what kind of device (laptop, tablet, mobile, iPod) you use to send a message, as your messages log will be accessible from each of your devices. It is very handy to be able to text from your laptop, and continue the conversation on your smartphone. iMessage also offers a group communication feature.

Social networks
- ☐ Twitter
- ☐ Facebook
- ☐ Path

Twitter lets you share messages of no more than 140 characters with the entire world, as well as send private messages. This service enables you to follow interesting people and stay on top of the latest news, find articles on any subject, share knowledge, ask questions, and let the world know what you are doing. Facebook is a social network through which you can let people know what's on your mind both in your personal and your professional life, as well as share fun content, send instant messages, and work together in groups.

Path presents itself as the place to be for your private life, allowing you to share 'moments' with a maximum of 150 people. On Path, you can share messages with one person, with a group, or publicly. Messages include text and voice messages, photos, videos, stickers, but also updates on what music you're listening to, what book you're reading, where you are, and when you are asleep. You can use small icons, such as a 'smile' or 'heart', to signify the emotions triggered by messages posted by others. This platform gives you insight into who has seen your updates, so that you can follow up on them offline. Another benefit of Path is that it lets you repost messages on other social media.

Update sharing and tracking
- ☐ Flipboard
- ☐ Scoop.it
- ☐ HootSuite
- ☐ IFTTT

Struggling to update all these different channels separately? If so, take a look at HootSuite, which lets you post a message to multiple social media with one click of a button. Finding it hard to filter Twitter and Facebook messages? Try using the Flipboard app on your tablet to organize your social media messages in a newspaper-like format. You could also make and share your own online magazine of interesting articles using Scoop.it. If you stick to a specific subject area for your magazine, you can share it with like-minded people or look for other similar magazines.[37]

Want to create smart combinations of your online tools? If so, If This Then That (IFTTT) is the tool you are looking for. This tool will automatically save your favorite tweets in Evernote, or save Facebook pictures that you have been tagged in to Dropbox.

Blogging
- ☐ Tumblr
- ☐ WordPress

Blogging is an ideal way of sharing knowledge. You can use blog posts to answer questions and share text, videos, images, and quotes. Used by numerous companies to share knowledge and boost brand awareness, blogging platforms Tumblr and WordPress are also highly popular among young people for daily updates on what they are doing. A blog is also a handy classroom resource that allows teachers to, for example, collate a portfolio of subjects covered in class or share interesting videos and articles. Publishing companies use blogs to draw attention to books they have coming out.

Visual communication

- ☐ Snapchat
- ☐ Vine
- ☐ Instagram
- ☐ Pinterest
- ☐ YouTube
- ☐ Vimeo
- ☐ ooVoo

Communicating through an audiovisual channel instead of through text is extremely popular in today's world. Tools that facilitate this kind of communication are therefore rapidly gaining ground. Instagram is a social network where you choose who to follow and share photos and videos with the entire world or privately. Vine is a tool that lets you make six-second videos to share on social media. The Snapchat photo messaging app enables users to share a moment in the 'here and

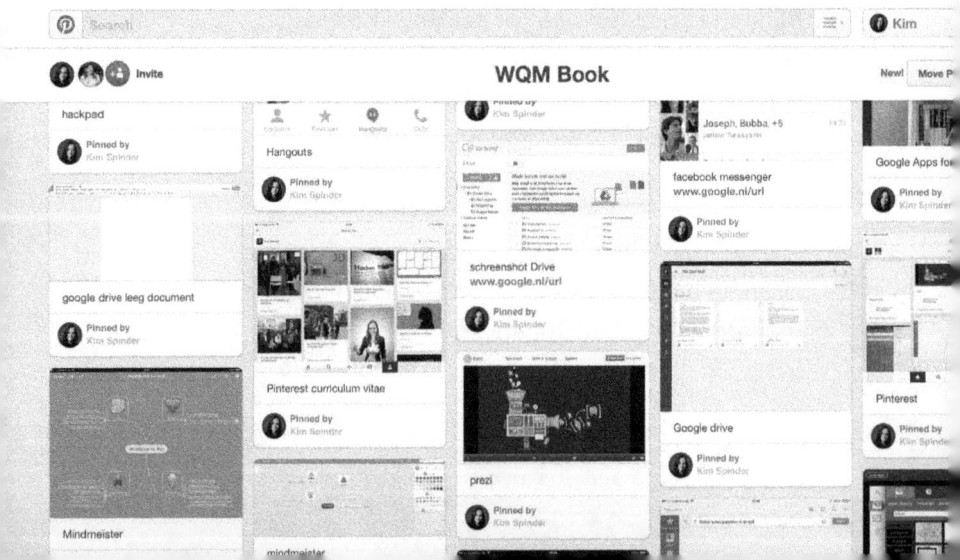

now' by snapping a picture or shooting video, adding a caption or drawing, and sending it to one or multiple persons in real time. This photo or video will self-destruct between 1 and 10 seconds later. A Snapchat Story remains available for only 24 hours. I use Snapchat to quickly share amusing things, such as a photo of a meeting that is going particularly well. On Pinterest, you can make collages of photos based on a specific subject (theme, product, or your company). You can also pin your resumé and recipes to your Pinterest board, as well as work together on presentations or magazines by jointly populating a board. I also use it for briefings for designers, as a kind of mood board with examples, pictures of the kind of atmosphere I am after for a certain design, and other kinds of inspiration. You can either keep the board private or make it accessible to the public. The ooVoo platform lets you have video conferences with a maximum of twelve friends, or send each other videos.

Video
- ☐ YouTube
- ☐ Vimeo
- ☐ PowToon
- ☐ Animoto

Another communication option is to make a video and put it on YouTube or Vimeo. PowToon lets you make an animation, while Animoto is a video creation service that uses photos and text.

Graphic communication

- ☐ Piktochart
- ☐ Infogr.am
- ☐ ComicLife

An infographic is an effective way of presenting information graphically. Using an infographic, you can capture your message in a visual presentation and share it through social media. You can make an infographic yourself using Piktochart or Infogr.am. There are also apps available that let you capture your message in comic book format, such as ComicLife.

Exit

You now know what kind of tools you need and what is available on the market. You have completed all the steps in the run-up to that big

THE EMAIL DIET.

100% HAPPY RESULTS.

E-TOX.
#WQM

leap. Don't hesitate, just go for it. It's better to make the wrong move and correct it later than to be assured a life that doesn't focus on your strengths and deprives you of ultimate control of what you do.

4

Join We Quit eMail

Quitting email will force you to think about why you do things the way you do. When you are busy, you never get round to asking yourself that, while that is precisely when you should be questioning your working methods. You can only experience the benefits of quitting email by actually doing it.

You will only get it when you have figured it out.
JOHAN CRUYFF

Just jump in at the deep end. Emmaly Sibbes: 'It's good to trigger yourself and step out of your comfort zone. It will open a lot of new doors to you. Go crazy, what do you have to lose?'

Results

WQM offers considerable rewards. So much time is lost on email. To me personally, WQM brought a major boost to my productivity: instead of four, I can now supervise forty projects. Others who have signed up to WQM have had the same experience: 'Everyone knows a lot of time is lost on email,' says Lucien Engelen.[38]

'I'm convinced that the effectiveness and time savings of cutting down on email will eclipse the effect of all Lean projects that companies have run to boost efficiency.'

The first results of WQM are so encouraging that companies should be advised to at least look into it. Especially when you consider that email produces a lot of stress, noise, and unproductivity.

Many people acknowledge that, but still stick with email. 'That's bizarre, something I really don't understand. Somehow, email gives them a solid footing, routine, and structure,' according to Kevin Weijers.

Quitting email goes beyond merely using social networks in the workplace. It's about trust, leadership, and autonomy. The biggest challenge of quitting email is not to never open your inbox again, but to let go: 'You need to trust your people and take a step back to let employees make their own decisions based on information that is shared openly and transparently,' says Marnix Bolkestein. 'As soon as you start seeing more creativity, better results, and happier staff, you know it's been worthwhile.'

Fail = First Attempt in Learning

Courage and perseverance

Employees who want to join the We Quit eMail movement need courage to venture off the beaten track, and break free of fixed routines. Quitting email is, after all, abandoning the traditional way of working. Although this will sometimes lead to an internal struggle, it does not mean you have to conform to the idea of 'this is just how we do things.' For WQM participants, this is certainly not a reason to throw in the towel. 'You just have to be creative, show initiative, and achieve results, people will then automatically start believing in it. After all, we are going forward in time, not backward. I, as a manager, do not shy away from that,' says Marnix Bolkestein.

The end of email?

Email is deeply rooted in organizations, and many employees cannot imagine their work without it. And yet, more and more employees are coming up against the limitations of email. It is impossible to do your job well when you have to deal with hundreds of emails every week.

Will email still be around in ten years' time? Views on that differ. The fact is that today's generation barely uses email. Instead, they communicate through WhatsApp, WeChat, Skype, and Facebook Messenger, or they share photos and videos through apps such as Vine, Instagram, and Snapchat.

IT expert Guus Pijpers thinks that email will still be around in ten years. 'Most companies have organized all their communications through email. It will take more than ten years to dismantle that structure.'[39]

Although a lot of people are curious about quitting email, they also want to still be able to communicate in the old way. In practice, it turns out that those who have made the leap never want to go back. Once you have gotten used to the new way of working, it is actually very hard to go back to email-based collaboration. 'I cannot imagine ever using email again for communications within my department or for projects. There comes a time when you simply see no other way,' says Marnix Bolkestein. 'You have to start somewhere, and quitting email makes a fine first step. Eventually, you end up with a new way of collaborating and organizing, one that gets far more out of collaborations. Unfortunately, email is still the communication standard at many organizations, but it simply doesn't work anymore. I can't wait for our way of working to become the norm.'

'I don't think I could do it, go back to email,' says Lucien Engelen. 'I would go nuts, and I would probably be asking myself every day what on earth I was doing. I also think I would get angry whenever I saw a colleague send an email to sixty people.'

Will you join us?

WQM constitutes a radical break from the past, and is an important step toward modernization. Do you have the courage to take the first step?

If you really care about starting a movement, have the courage to follow and show others how to follow. And when you find a lone nut doing something great, have the guts to be the first one to stand up and join in.

DEREK SIVERS, AUTHOR OF *ANYTHING YOU WANT*[40]

The more people join, the more people will follow, which will lead to the We Quit eMail movement snowballing into something big. Will you take the first step within 48 hours after reading this book? Joining is easy, here's how:

1. Get started with We Quit eMail, switch to other tools.
2. Become an ambassador. Support us on Facebook, Twitter, Google+, LinkedIn, Instagram and wequitmail.com.
3. Tweet your first step, using the hashtag #wqm.
4. Spread the word, tell people about your experiences.
5. Post tips on social media or one of the WQM platforms.

There is no passion to be found playing small — in settling for a life that is less than the one you are capable of living.

NELSON MANDELA

What if...

...the Internet is down

Luckily, quitting email is not purely about the digital highway, the technology, but also about the way we are connected to each other. Stopping by someone's desk or cubicle, having a coffee together, or picking up the phone are ideal ways of connecting people. Consider it a great opportunity! And whenever the Internet is down, there will be far more important things to worry about. Besides, email would also be down.

...I have to apply for a job by email

This is a kind of situation that requires creativity and an ability to put yourself in the other's shoes. I always check, for example, whether the company where I'm applying for a job is active on social media. If so, chances are that they will, in fact, appreciate you submitting your application through social media. More and more vacancies are posted on LinkedIn, allowing you to apply immediately. But there's another fine opportunity for the taking here: try to drastically change your ways.

Once, when I was bidding for a contract, I made a huge poster to land that contract. On the front I had written an engaging quote, so as to make sure they would put up the poster. My pitch for the contract was on the back. I had the poster hand-delivered to their office to make sure my message stood out and allow the recipient to unwrap it at his or her earliest convenience. I figured they would probably not appreciate me spontaneously turning up in person with a big poster. Try to make choices that suit you as a person, be creative, and tailor your communication methods to the recipient.

...my colleagues don't want to

It often happens that one or two colleagues do not want to join in. They dig in their heels and refuse to create an account and communicate through social media. Start by launching a pilot with those people who do want to join in. Persevere and do not give up when you turn out to be the only one posting messages. Colleagues who refuse to join in will often come round when they hear how handy it is or when they feel that they are out of the loop. When they hear someone say: 'It was on Basecamp,'

they become curious and create an account.
They don't want to be left out.

.my colleagues lack the skills

The absence of online skills is a serious
problem at companies. Not all employees
can work with the new tools; some need
help choosing and getting familiarized with
the tools. Although this group of computer
illiterates does want to join in, they need
help in overcoming the technology threshold.
Organize training sessions for them, explain-
ing how social media work, and allowing
them to practice and brainstorm together
about how to use social media in their day-
to-day activities.

.my colleagues don't get it

We Quit eMail challenges you to rethink how
you collaborate and communicate. When
you have not yet experienced the alternative
options, it will be hard to understand the difference. A much-heard counter-argument is:
'You are only moving information to another
place; everything stays the same, and you will
only be more inconvenienced because you
have to check more platforms.' WQM is not a
crusade against email, but rather against the
way it is used. It is not up to you to persuade
everyone, but you can get people excited. Try
to tempt them to work differently and experience the difference for themselves. Each

and every one of the experiences of people who have regained control of their work thanks to WQM is positive. These people also say they never expected these results beforehand.

...I don't feel like using all these new tools

Although it depends on your work environment, you will also get very far without all these new tools. There are examples of companies that have introduced a quick fifteen-minute stand-up meeting at the start of the day to discuss important issues. In the fifteen minutes following such a quick meeting, co-workers talk to each other about any remaining questions, often one on one whenever the matter is not relevant to the entire group, following which they are all set to be productive the rest of the day. Managers can have a 30-minute walk-in session every morning or make sure they are in their regular spot by the coffee machine at a specific time to enable employees to ask any questions they may have. There are also departments where staff have lunch together once or twice a week to ask questions and exchange information. Employees experience this as far more productive than sending hundreds of emails back and forth every day. Sit down with your team (or go visit everyone in the office) and come up with your own version.

...my colleagues continue to send emails alongside the online platform

Whenever they find themselves pressed for time, co-workers may suddenly revert to email out of a kind of fear of the message not getting to everyone on time. When that happens, post the information on the online platform you are using, and text group members asking them to check it and respond. If you were to draw attention to the information by email, half of the recipients would respond on the online platform, while the other half would respond by email, giving you two information flows. This is extremely inconvenient whenever you need to find information later. True, new work arrangements will help streamline this, but it is always a good idea to appoint someone to keep the group on its toes.

...we really cannot do without email

WQM is not an anti-email movement, but raises awareness of the way we are keeping each other locked in a digital stranglehold. Quitting email is not a goal in itself. As Lucien Engelen indicates: 'I, too, still send the occasional email now and again, to dignitaries or when there really is no other way, such as when contacting government offices.' You decide when to make an exception, such as for confidential documents. Some draw the line at no longer sending emails, but still receive e-bills, purchase confirmation emails, or verification emails. You decide how far you want to go.

...I suffer withdrawal symptoms

You are indeed likely to suffer withdrawal symptoms. Worse still, you are so accustomed to checking your email several times a day that it would be exceptional if you were *not* to suffer withdrawal symptoms. Keep a tally of how often you grab your cell phone to check your email and see how drastically this has reduced by the end of the week. It will help you focus on the things you want to achieve, and avoid getting distracted. Do not transfer your email addiction to continuously checking social media out of a fear of people forgetting about you, but instead concentrate on performing the tasks on your to-do list. Trust me, you will feel truly satisfied at the end of the day.

...I lose track of what has been said and where

They can make your head spin, all those tools. Did he reply on Twitter or through WhatsApp? Did I get that address in a text or in a Facebook message? I could, of course, say that it is easy to interconnect things using tools such as If This Then That, but I guess the last thing you want is yet another tool. I myself prevent information from getting lost by clearly agreeing on what to communicate where and with whom. I have agreed a preferred channel for most people. Only people who are just starting out often use multiple channels for the same kind of information. When you get into it, you become astute, and agree beforehand which channels to use. It is also important that you do not shy away from calling people to account when they deviate from such agreements. Whenever my secretary, for example, texts me about things that are not urgent, I tell her to use another channel. For me, texting is for urgent matters only, otherwise it would get too cluttered. And when that happens, it becomes difficult for me to filter out the really urgent matters, and that eventually makes her life more complicated as well. Sometimes I copy information to a place that is more logical within my range of communication platforms. This enables me to find the information when I need it later. And if you really cannot manage to streamline your platform usage, you will unfortunately have to look a little harder sometimes. But that's a problem that is quite common in the digital age.

...not everyone wants to join in – is it an everyone or no one kind of deal?

What if your superior refuses to quit email? What if other crucial team members don't want any part of it? Is that end of story or is there still hope? That is when people get creative. I have already seen people form small groups based on a mutual agreement to stop emailing each other. The great thing about such arrangements is that people are individually agreeing between themselves to quit email, creating a kind of ripple effect. The more people agree to stop emailing each other, the fewer emails will be sent across the company.

Such mutual agreements cease to apply as soon as someone becomes involved in the conversation who has not joined WQM. This ensures that WQM never poses a threat to those at the company who want to keep emailing.

...an external contact asks me to reply by email

Set up a clear automated reply in your out-of-office assistant, stating, for example, that you only read your email once a day. Specify an alternative channel, including one for urgent matters. Depending on your position, it may also prove helpful to emailers to put answers to frequently asked questions in an automatic reply. It is also part of our zeitgeist to expect people to reply quickly. The question is whether you should want to go along with that. This is a discussion I would very much like us to have.

Do you want to quit email altogether?

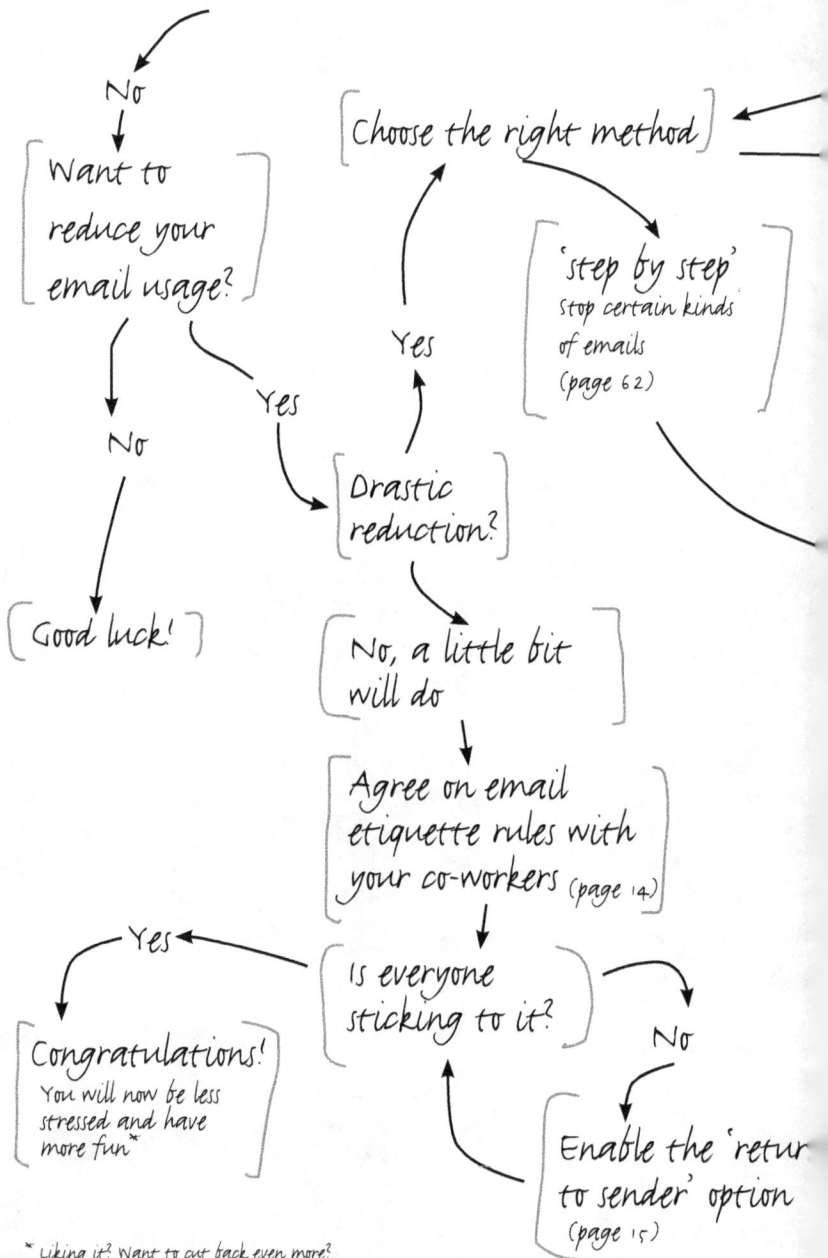

No

Want to reduce your email usage?

Choose the right method

'step by step'
stop certain kinds
of emails
(page 62)

Yes

Yes

No

Drastic reduction?

Yes

Good luck!

No, a little bit will do

Agree on email etiquette rules with your co-workers (page 14)

Yes

Is everyone sticking to it?

No

Congratulations!
You will now be less
stressed and have
more fun*

Enable the 'retur
to sender' option
(page 15)

* Liking it? Want to cut back even more?
Proceed with 'choose the right method.'

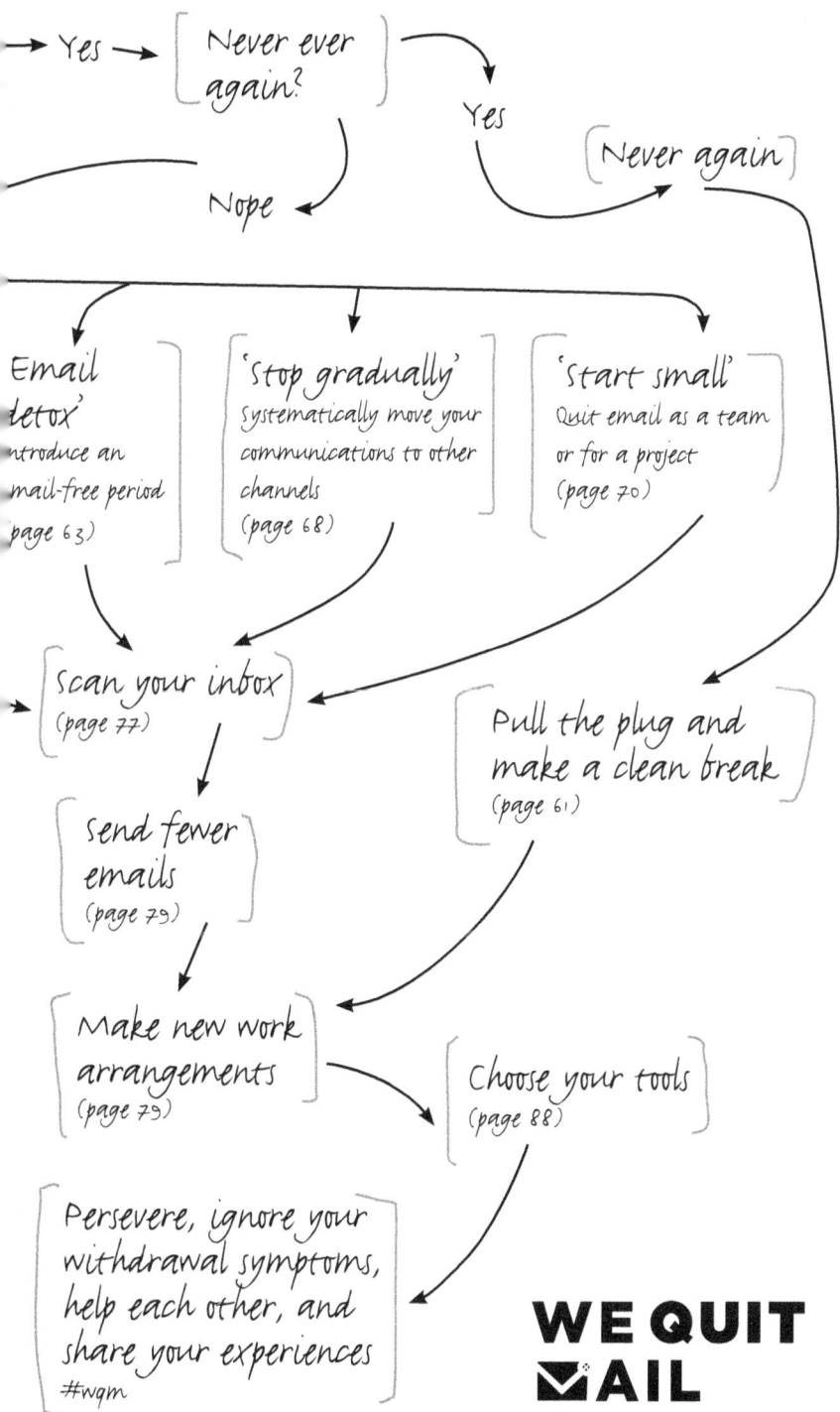

Yes → [Never ever again?]

Yes

[Never again]

Nope

[Email detox
Introduce an mail-free period (page 63)]

['stop gradually'
Systematically move your communications to other channels (page 68)]

['start small'
Quit email as a team or for a project (page 70)]

[Scan your inbox (page 77)]

[Pull the plug and make a clean break (page 61)]

[Send fewer emails (page 79)]

[Make new work arrangements (page 79)]

[Choose your tools (page 88)]

[Persevere, ignore your withdrawal symptoms, help each other, and share your experiences #wqm]

WE QUIT ✉AIL

Sources

- 'E-TOX', *Volkskrant Magazine*, 22 februari 2014
- 'Stop er nou es mee', http://lucienengelen. wordpress.com/2014/02/22/stop-er-nou-es-mee/
- 'Did Google just kill e-mail?', www.twistimage. com/blog/archives/did-google-just-kill-email/
- 'Stoppen met e-mail', www.pm.nl/artikel/2992/ stoppenmet-e-mail
- 'Ik stap een jaar uit het bombardement van de e-mails', www.tijd.be/r/t/1/id/9468366
- 'Why Leaders Eat Last', http://vimeo. com/79899786
- 'Why we use email for everything and how we can be better emailers', http://thenextweb. com/entrepreneur/2014/02/03/ use-email-everything-can-betteremailers/
- 'How to get a busy person to respond to your email. 5 rules for good email etiquette', https://medium.com/a-path-to-efficiency/ 52e5d4d69671
- 'Een tweetje voor het slapengaan: de impact van technologie op je nachtrust', www.frank-watching.com/archive/2014/02/22/ een-tweetje-voor-het-slapengaan-deimpact-van-technologie-op-je-nachtrust-infographic
- 'Inbox 10,000: Some Thoughts After A Month Away From Email', http://techcrunch. com/2011/08/02/inbox-10000/
- 'The sad truth', www.emilymagazine. com/?p=371
- 'I'm quitting e-mail', http://techcrunch. com/2011/07/06/i-wouldnt-say-ive-been-missing-it/
- 'Email Is The New Pony Express — And It's

Time To Put It Down', www.fastcompany.
com/3002170/email-newpony-express-and-its-
time-put-it-down

☐ 'comScore's 2012 U.S. Digital Future in Focus',
www.neowin.net/news/webmail-shows-
massive-declines

☐ 'Email Takes Up 28% of Workers' Time'
http://mashable.com/2012/08/01/email-
workers-time/

☐ 'Email Statistics Report 2011-2015', www.
radicati.com/wp/wpcontent/uploads/2011/05/
Email-Statistics-Report-2011-2015-Execu-
tive-Summary.pdf

☐ 'The social economy: Unlocking value and
productivity through social technologies',
www.mckinsey.com/insights/high_tech_
telecoms_internet/the_social_economy

☐ 'Why we use email for everything and how we
can be better emailers', http://thenextweb.
com/entrepreneur/2014/02/03/
use-email-everything-can-betteremailers/

☐ 'Productivity Hacks: More Talk, Less Type',
www.linkedin.com/today/post/article/
20140121112531-5935179-productivity-
hacksmore-talk-less-type

☐ 'I Banned All Internal E-Mails at My Company
for a Week', www.forbes.com/sites/forbes-
leadershipforum/2012/10/25/i-banned-all-in-
ternal-e-mails-at-mycompany-for-a-week/#

☐ 'Disruptions: Looking for Relief From a Flood
of Email', http://bits.blogs.nytimes.
com/2014/01/19/disruptionslooking-for-relief-
from-a-flood-of-email/?_php=true&_
type=blogs&_php=true&_type=blogs&_r=1

- 'To Reduce E-mail, Get Execs to Send Fewer Messages', http://blogs.hbr.org/2013/09/research-to-reduce-emailload/
- 'To Reduce E-mail, Start at the Top', http://hbr.org/2013/09/to-reduce-e-mail-start-at-the-top/ar/1
- 'Dropbox CEO: The creators of email would "cry" if they foresaw its slow evolution', www.citeworld.com/cloud/22697/dropbox-drew-houston-marc-benioff-dreamforce
- 'Civil servants to abandon "time thief" email for a day', www.telegraph.co.uk/news/politics/10395039/Civil-servants-to-abandon-time-thief-email-for-a-day.html?utm_source=buffer&utm_campaign=Buffer&utm_content=buffer09efd&utm_medium=twitter
- 'A World Without Email', www.elsua.net/2010/08/25/aworld-without-email-%E2%80%94-year-3-weeks-24-to-28-email-is-where-knowledge-goes-to-die-the-presentation/

Notes

1   http://tedxnijmegen.nl/2013/04/kim-spinder-first-fol-
    lowers-wanted-lets-quit-email/

2   www.citeworld.com/cloud/22697/dropbox-drew-hou-
    ston-marc-benioff-dreamforce

3   http://thenextweb.com/entrepreneur/2014/02/03/
    useemail-everything-can-better-emailers/

4   http://hbr.org/2013/06/e-mail-not-dead-evolving/ar/1

5   http://bits.blogs.nytimes.com/2014/01/19/disruptions-
    looking-for-relief-from-a-flood-of-email/?_php=true&_
    type=blogs&_php=true&_type=blogs&_r=1

6   www.frankwatching.com/archive/2014/02/22/
    een-tweetje-voor-het-slapengaan-de-impact-van-tech-
    nologie-opje-nachtrust-infographic

7   http://nl.wikipedia.org/wiki/Getting_Things_Done

8   www.paulgraham.com/ambitious.html

9   Watch this YouTube video to see how this works: www.
    youtube.com/watch?v=QIqA_YKeboc

10 http://bits.blogs.nytimes.com/2014/01/19/disruptions-
    looking-for-relief-from-a-flood-of-email/?_php=true&_
    type=blogs&_php=true&_type=blogs&_r=1

11 www.emilymagazine.com/?p=371

12 www.ghorhm.nl/organisatie/ghor-bureau/
    medewerkers-2/

13 http://hbr.org/2013/06/e-mail-not-dead-evolving/ar/1

14 www.mckinsey.com/insights/high_tech_telecoms_
    internet/the_social_economy

15 http://mashable.com/2012/08/01/email-workers-time/

16 http://hbr.org/2013/06/e-mail-not-dead-evolving/ar/1

17 http://hbr.org/2013/09/to-reduce-e-mail-start-at-
    thetop/ar/1

18 http://blogs.hbr.org/2013/09/research-to-reduce-email-
    load/

19 www.linkedin.com/today/post/article/20130512003857-
    19886490-12-500-hours-of-reading-emails-every-
    month?trk=mp-reader-card

20 Members of the network discussed these issues in a
    closed discussion forum on Facebook. The outcome of
    the discussion was further fleshed out and detailed in
    meetings. This eventually became the basis for the
    signals issued by jongGR. http://2013.jonggrmagazine.
    nl/#!1-Cover

21 www.open-lab.nl

22 http://bits.blogs.nytimes.com/2014/01/19/disruptions-
    looking-for-relief-from-a-flood-of-email/?_php=true&_
    type=blogs&_php=true&_type=blogs&_r=1

23 www.tijd.be/r/t/1/id/9468366

24 www.ted.com/talks/sherry_turkle_alone_together.html
    and http://programma.vpro.nl/gesprekop2/aflever-
    ingen/2011/aflevering3-sherry-turkle.html

25 www.startwithwhy.com/default.aspx

26 www.linkedin.com/today/post/article/20140121112531-
    5935179-productivity-hacks-more-talk-less-type

27 http://thenextweb.com/entrepreneur/2014/02/03/
    useemail-everything-can-better-emailers/

28 www.lifehacking.nl en http://lifehacking.nl/productivi-
    teit-2/video-wat-is-lifehacking/

29 www.forbes.com/sites/forbesleadershipfo-
    rum/2012/10/25/i-banned-all-internal-e-mails-at-my-
    company-for-a-week/#

30 www.telegraph.co.uk/news/politics/10395039/Civil-
    servants-to-abandon-time-thief-email-for-a-day.
    html?utm_source=buffer&utm_campaign=Buff-
    er&utm_content=buffer09efd&utm_medium=twitter

31 www.gov.uk/government/organisations/cabinet-office
    and www.gov.uk/government/people/stephen-kelly--2

32 http://techcrunch.com/2011/08/02/inbox-10000/

33 https://plus.google.com/communities

34 Did Google just kill e-mail? www.twistimage.com/blog/
    archives/did-google-just-kill-email/

35 www.teamwork.com/ and www.huddle.com/

36 www.christinehueber.com/which-of-the-top-5-profes-
    sional-networking-sites-linkedin-quora-plaxo-viadeo-
    xing-is-best-for-your-business-by-christine-hueber/

37 www.scoop.it/t/we-quit-mail

38 'E-TOX', *Volkskrant Magazine*, 22 February 2014

39 ibid.

40 www.youtube.com/watch?v=V74AxCqOTvg

www.ingramcontent.com/pod-product-compliance
Lightning Source LLC
Chambersburg PA
CBHW031944190326
41519CB00007B/649